Georgia Hinterleitner

Small Stones to Fill Big Pictures

A Look at Contemporary Ethnocultural and Regional Canadian Children's Picturebooks, Their Figures and Themes

Reflections

Literatures in English
outside Britain and the USA

Albert-Reiner Glaap (Ed.)

Band 22

Georgia Hinterleitner

Small Stones to Fill Big Pictures

A Look at Contemporary Ethnocultural and Regional Canadian Children's Picturebooks, Their Figures and Themes

WVT Wissenschaftlicher Verlag Trier

Hinterleitner, Georgia: Small Stones to Fill Big Pictures:
A Look at Contemporary Ethnocultural and Regional Canadian
Children's Picturebooks, Their Figures and Themes /
Georgia Hinterleitner. –
Trier : WVT Wissenschaftlicher Verlag Trier, 2012
(Reflections. Literatures in English
outside Britain and the USA ; Bd. 22)
ISBN 978-3-86821-404-8

Diese Publikation wurde mit finanzieller Unterstützung
aus den Fördermitteln des Vizerektorats für Forschung
der Leopold-Franzens-Universität Innsbruck gedruckt.
Sie wurde ursprünglich am Institut für Anglistik der
Leopold-Franzens-Universität Innsbruck als Diplomarbeit
eingereicht.

Cover art by Mary Huang
http://humangray.com/

Cover design: Brigitta Disseldorf

ISBN 978-3-86821-404-8

WVT Wissenschaftlicher Verlag Trier
Bergstraße 27, 54295 Trier
Postfach 4005, 54230 Trier
Tel.: (0651) 41503 / 9943344, Fax: 41504
Internet: http://www.wvttrier.de
E-Mail: wvt@wvttrier.de

To Helga, for all her guidance and encouragement.

To Kim, Elaine, Flidget, Steffi, Mary and Gina, for having my back through everything.

To Gudrun, for being.

Table of Contents

List of Tables and Figures

1. Introduction

"You have to write the book that wants to be written. And if the book will be too difficult for grown-ups, then you write it for children,"[1] Madeleine L'Engle says, in what is perhaps a slightly tongue-in-cheek jab at the status of children's literature in the Western world of today. Almost four hundred years have passed since the first writings for an audience of children began to emerge, and nearly forty years since academics and criticism slowly started to turn their attention to children's books as a subject of study. From its tentative beginnings, children's literature has blossomed into a verdant jungle, whose many branches bring forth an even greater number of different fruits. And yet, its status remains an ambivalent one, simultaneously dismissed because of its primary target audience, and closely watched for the same reasons. No other field of literature, no other kind of writer, is faced with so many challenges and concerns — is the book helpful? Is the book harmful? Too complex? Too frightening? Or too dismissive of values? Many of these questions, and the judgments that follow in their wake, are spurred by the image of childhood which resides in the adult mind, a representation of a state — for it tends to be perceived as a state — that remains only partially accessible through scattered memories. Some look back on it with nostalgic fondness, some with anger, some with fascination, still others scarcely look back on it at all, and yet it is all these different attitudes and subsequent conceptions that play a role when it comes to writing for children. The author, the publisher, the critic, and the adult who eventually decides to buy or not buy a certain book all draw on their own notions of what constitutes childhood and all the weight attached to it — propriety, education, and entertainment. Canada is a country that has managed to achieve a high level of quality and variety in the production and promotion of children's books in a much shorter amount of time than most other Western nations. Slow to emerge from the shadow of colonialism, its literature has come to reflect a distinct sense of nationality while at the same time developing to try and reflect the many voices, stories, and concerns of its citizens, whose roots can be found in many different places in the world. Naturally, children's books have not remained unaffected by this phenome-

---

1 Madeleine L'Engle, qtd. in Denney.

non. Especially picturebooks, with their unique combination of text and image, provide a wealth of insight into the themes that preoccupy Canada as a nation and communicate these themes to Canadian children. This thesis will discuss these new Canadian children's picturebooks which have come to portray regional or ethnocultural aspects in their narratives, the problems and developments they focus on, and also the many representations of childhood they offer. By tracing the argument from the general to the specific, starting with the constructedness of childhood and its effect on children's books in general, before moving on to the forces and developments that have shaped Canadian children's literature into what it is today (or perhaps, what it is *at the moment*, for no aspect of literature is a process to a definite end), it will pave the way for an analysis of a select number of contemporary Canadian children's picturebooks with a regional or ethnocultural focus, and the themes to be found therein.

2. Framework

In order to speak about children's books, it is first necessary to examine various issues that dominate the field. Several of these factors have shaped children's books, their production and critical treatment for a very long time, perhaps even since the beginning. Unlike any other field of literature, any other genre or writing for a specific group, children's books are largely not produced by members of the same group as the primary target audience: the children. This central difference has very complex consequences, such as the fact that the disposition of the adult who is in control, be they writer, reader, or critic, depends on a construct of what childhood means, what it is like, and what kinds of abilities children should be granted versus the abilities they do have. These constructs, varied as they are, also influence what should be considered a children's book, how writing for children should be categorized, and how published child writers, rarer though they are, are perceived. Furthermore, the controlling power exercised by adults has consequences for the creation of children's texts themselves. Since the adult is so integral to the reception of children's literature — after all, it is adult guardians who evaluate books and decide to spend money to buy them (thus keeping the writers in business) — children's literature is required to address a dual audience. This is fundamentally different from the way literature with no particular target audience operates, since children's literature is charged with not only tailoring the texts, the themes and illustrations specifically to young readers, but is made to turn to a very different audience for approval and support at the same time, namely an audience working with assumptions about childhood and the pressure of being good parents or good teachers, who act 'in children's best interest.' This also affects how children's own voices are factored into the process, whether their opinions are considered, accepted, or valued, whether they are allowed to exercise their very different comprehension mechanisms and pose the questions they want to pose, and whether or not their likes and dislikes are respected. The following chapters will examine these points in detail in order to provide a measure of understanding of just how complex the mechanisms surrounding children's books are.

2.1. Through the Funhouse Mirror: Childhood as a Construct

In many ways, trying to arrive at a satisfactory definition of childhood is slightly akin to attempting a definition of a Rorschach inkblot test. Although there are certain physical factors that permit an approximation to the inkblot and what it depicts — the paper, the ink, its color, the degree of wetness and how far it has spread — in the end, what the inkblot truly represents is a matter of individual interpretation, as imagination, experience, and memory come into play to make sense of the shape on the paper. Naturally, different people can arrive at the same conclusion; the shape looks like a butterfly, some might say, while others will identify a cloud, and others still, a bunny. And just as the Rorschach inkblot causes people to think of different images, so is the concept of childhood colored by different expectations and points of view.

There are numerous ways in which one can approach the concept of childhood. One is the purely biological perspective, which, similar to the physical attributes of the inkblot, attempts to find quantifiable elements to use as defining aspects. In this case, childhood is defined via the factors of age and growth. Although this seems straightforward enough, difficulties soon arise when it comes to the application of terms. Definitions tend to vary depending on where one draws the line. Some distinguish between childhood and adolescence, using the onset of sexual development as a line of separation between the two. Some choose to add 'infancy' to the list of stages, distinguishing between very early childhood and later childhood. Still others choose to forego these distinctions, thereby describing the entire period of time with all its changes as 'childhood.' However, regardless of the precise points in time used to stake out the concept of childhood against sub- or sister-concepts, it is perhaps most useful to turn to the subject of growth itself, rather than the degree or length of growth. Growth implies changes, implies movement, so one could describe childhood as a period of constant flux, biological specifications altering from one moment to the next.

Psychology expands on the concept of growth by adding a mental dimension to the purely physical development. A child's cognitive powers and personality develop over time as it begins to acquire certain skills, thus childhood is a time of learning and experimentation that is characterized by large leaps in cognitive ability and skill. Over time, various models have been devised to monitor and analyze children's psychological development and determine phases in which they acquire new skills. Jean Piaget's theory of cognitive development remains one of the most influential works,[2] proposing four broad stages of cognitive growth in children from birth to twelve years and onward:

- The sensorimotor period, lasting from birth to two years of age, in which children move beyond reflex activity such as grasping and sucking to acquire sensorimotor skills and object permanence.[3]
- The preoperational period, lasting from two years to seven years, in which children begin to develop language skills, the ability to reason, and which is characterized by what Piaget named "egocentrism,"[4] in other words, the child's difficulty at distinguishing between subjective and objective reality.[5]
- The concrete operational period, lasting from seven to eleven years, in which children begin to cooperate and compete with others, developing moral judgment and logical thought.[6]
- And the formal operational period, starting at around age twelve, which is characterized by increasingly abstract thinking and advanced formal logic.[7]

The model has not been without critique, and there is disagreement on the point in time at which developmental leaps should happen, permitting only a general framework. However, the fact remains that childhood is the period of time in which human beings undergo the most important steps in their cognitive development and acquire critical skills that allow them to perceive and interact with the world around them.

---

2 Herbert Ginsburg, and Sylvia Opper, *Piaget's Theory of Intellectual Development*, 2nd ed. (Englewood Cliffs: Prentice-Hall, 1979) xi.

3 Ginsburg and Opper 26-68.

4 Ginsburg and Opper 97.

5 Ginsburg and Opper 69-112.

6 Ginsburg and Opper 69-112.

7 Ginsburg and Opper 178-205.

For the sake of completeness, it seems worth noting that psychologists also use another concept that is only tangentially related to childhood itself: the so-called 'second childhood,' a term used to describe the state of dementia and associated shifts in behavior and judgment in elderly people. At first glance, this seems to be a rather innocuous figure of speech, whereby a similarity is construed between phenomena that are actually rather dissimilar. The English language is full of expressions such as this one, yet "second childhood" deserves a closer examination, as it allows a glimpse of how perceptions of childhood influence our lives. Applying the term 'childhood' as a euphemism to what is, in no uncertain terms, a process of mental decay and loss of control in an adult person presents a rather startling contrast to the relative neutrality that normally pertains to the term. The likening of the behavior and state of mind of the young and growing to an illness characterized by erratic behavior and limited judgment radically transforms and contests established notions of childhood. It causes certain attributes of the child, normally perceived as perfectly natural, to appear pathological. In the event, developmental patterns (such as the child's initial lack of a critical distance to itself) come to be seen as symptoms of an aberration. As a result, "childhood" moves into semantic proximity of words such as 'childish,' which describes unrestrained, disruptive behavior and, ironically, has no counterpart. No one will be chastised for being too 'adultish.' In the light of these facts, one almost feels compelled to ask the question of whether the transition from childhood to adulthood is marked by the reduction or elimination of undesirable qualities.

The sociological perspective defines children as beings in the care of and under supervision by adults, who feed and protect, guide and teach them, establish and enforce rules of conduct so as to enable them to survive in human society. Here, childhood is a period of time when human beings are guided by their fully grown counterparts to become functional, independent adults. It is perhaps this point that underscores the relationship between children and adults, and the underlying power dynamics, the most. Adults have power over children in a plurality of ways, and in almost every aspect of their lives. In and of itself, this power is nothing negative — most social groups, be they human or animal, adhere to certain hierarchical structures to uphold order and stay functional. Within these organizations, the young occupy a status that is both privileged and restricted. They are protected and cared for, yet are expected to adhere to many regulations. However, especially in contemporary human societies, these power dynamics have become extremely layered and complex, and also subject to change. In "Constructs of Childhood: Constructs of Self," Sorin and Galloway compile a table of different power structures that list ten different power relationships between adults and children.

Table 1: Constructs of Children: Constructs of Self

Image of child	Image of adult	Power of child	Power of adult
Child as innocent Carefree, good, incompetent, vulnerable, ignorant, naïve, a blank slate.	**The adult as protector** Loving and caring nurturers of children who act in the 'child's best interest'.	Little power.	A lot of power from their (assumed) capacity to guide and protect children and limit the child's environment.
Child as evil Original sin; innate evil 'an untamed threat' (Corsaro 1997), destructive; threat to the social order; driven by their own needs, desires and pleasures.	**The adult as good/moral** Controllers of children. Adults have gone from an evil stage to a more mature stage — they are 'good' and keepers of moral order.	Children have little power since they are 'driven'.	Adults have power to control the child (as opposed to the environment, above).
The snowballing child Seems to be in charge of the adults around them. Makes inflexible demands of adults for their own short term gratification.	**The deferring adult** Does not set limits therefore opportunity to negotiate power and autonomy is denied.	The child has illegitimate power — they get a little power and it snowballs.	Could have power, but they hand their power, authority and influence over to the child.

The out-of-control child Uses power in a negative way, for example by being violent, to get the parent to do what they want them to do. Eventually they feel out of control as if no-one is there to help them regain their control.	**The ineffectual adult** Feels defeated by the child. Feels as if they have little power and influence and/or do not know how to regain influence with the child.	Power is used in a negative way by the child. When the child is not sanctioned, they eventually feel out of control.	Their power is ineffectual. They feel defeated by the child.
The noble/saviour child Beautiful and beloved, can save people, look after others, e.g. Jesus, Harry Potter.	**The dependent adult** The adult depends on the child to get their needs/wants met.	Power is assumed through circums-tances. The child is neither agentic nor innocent.	Adults absolve them-selves of respon-sibility or literally cannot undertake that which is ex-pected of them (by the child, by society, by themselves).
The miniature adult Children are the same as adults.	**The adult** The mature being.	Power of the child lies in the capacity to learn and participate in a world that is constructed for them by adults. The child is less knowing.	Power lies in their capacity to harness the abilities of the child to suit adult imperatives. Adults can be tyrannical or loving guides. Adults are knowledgeable.
The adult-in-training Human 'becomings' rather than human 'beings' (Hutchinson & Charlesworth 2000). Have future potential.	**The teacher**		
The commodified child Child is an object to be used and con-sumed by adults.	**The self-interested adult** Adult exploits the child for economic gain.	The child is power-less although they may have illusionary power as their image is manipulated by adults.	Hold the majority of power.

The child as victim Children of famine, pandemic diseases, war and poverty.	**The absent adult** The child's significant adults lack power. Adults who do have power turn a blind eye to what is happening to children.	Powerless.	Powerless.
The agentic child Capable and competent. An optimistic construct. Rather than 'becoming', the child is a social actor (James, Jenks & Prout 1998).	**Co-constructor of being** Helps the child on their life journey, as the child helps the adult on their journey.	Power is negotiated and shared.	Power is negotiated and shared. The adult lends their power, strength and resources with the child rather than imposing on the child.

Source: Sorin, R. and G. Galloway, "Constructs of Childhood: Constructs of Self," *Children Australia* 31.2 (2006): 21.

Examining this table, two points become apparent. Firstly, the power relationships identified by Sorin and Galloway are self-perpetuating. In other words, once established and solidified, particularly in a pan-societal context, they are very difficult to change or erode. Secondly, each power dynamic has a construct of childhood as its base, an assumption on which the dynamic is built. A particular outlook on childhood will give rise to the corresponding power structure, and this subsequently influences ideas about children's capacities, intentions, and states of mind.

Three of these constructs stand out in particular, since they have dominated the Western view of childhood historically: the miniature adult, who is viewed as no different from 'grown' adults, the evil child who is born from a sinful act and must have this inherited sin forcibly removed, and the innocent child, whose mind is a blank slate to be filled and shaped by adults.[8] Perhaps the earliest view one can retrace historically is that of the child as a

8 Reesa Sorin, "Changing Images of Childhood — Reconceptualising Early Childhood Practice," *International Journal of Transitions in Childhood* 1 (2005): 13.

miniature adult — in other words, there existed no specific notion of childhood as a separate state. In pre-industrial Europe, children were expected to do the same work and bear the same burdens as adults due to the high mortality rate and poor economic conditions.[9] The ideological outlook is prominently reflected in medieval and Renaissance portraiture, in which children were depicted with the same proportions, expressions and stance as adults.[10] Somewhat parallel to this construct runs the idea of the evil child, which is heavily colored by the influence of Christian religion, and which remained a dominant model until the 19th century. This attitude is still reflected in the works of 19th-century writers such as Charlotte Brontë or Charles Dickens, who tend to depict the child protagonist in a sympathetic light, yet often have adult characters react to them according to the notion of the evil child. For example, when the young Jane Eyre defends herself against an attack by her older stepbrother, the adult figures in the household respond by labeling this as a sign of the evil in the child, remarking upon her "wickedness" and calling for severe punishment.[11]

The construct of the innocent child is one that first began to gain popularity at the onset of the Industrial Revolution and the subsequent emergence of a new, wealthy middle class. The movement of Romanticism in particular, with its heavy emphasis on emotions and the subconscious, idealized childhood as a time of innocence and boundless imagination.[12] The child is eventually tainted by the rules of adults and adult society, losing its connection to the primal and the unrestrained. This view, though modified over the course of time, remains even today. Sorin remarks upon this by stating:

> In the early childhood classroom, this construct is visible in practices of censorship, or sheltering children from the real world. We metaphorically as well as literally cover children's eyes when images of violence, death or sexuality inadvertently present themselves in the media. The books, videos, games and activities we choose for children are often sanitised to present some aspects of life while

---

9 Peter Hunt, "Defining Children's Literature," *Only Connect: Readings on Children's Literature*, ed. Sheila Egoff, (Toronto: Oxford UP, 1996) 13.

10 Philippe Ariès, *Centuries of Childhood: A Social History of Family Life*, trans. Robert Baldick (New York: Vintage Books, 1962) 128.

11 Charlotte Brontë, *Jane Eyre* (1847. London: Penguin, 1994) 14.

12 Roni Natov, *The Poetics of Childhood* (New York: Routledge, 2006) 7.

> excluding others. For example, stories with witches or monsters are often excluded from early childhood bookshelves because, in the teacher's view, they might cause fear or anxiety in children.[13]

These three extreme and partly conflicting views alone serve to illustrate that the notion of childhood in the adult mind is just that — a notion. The adult concept of childhood is a construct, no matter the time period it exists in or its ever-changing attributes, and it is a construct that is unlikely to disappear, simply because as an adult, we have no choice but to summon a construct to aid us. "How close can we, as adults, get to the inner life, where the profusion of our memories lies?"[14] Roni Natov asks in *Poetics of Childhood*, describing the dilemma adults face simply by virtue of being adults. We are not aware of childhood as we live it. It is only later that we look back on our younger years, and attempt to piece together the children we must have been from our fragmented memories. The human brain is far from a perfect abacus, meticulously storing and categorizing the day-to-day experiences; rarely do we recall anything but an outstanding experience, and even more rarely is it retained in the manner in which it actually occurred — sometimes becoming rose-tinted with age, sometimes dramatized. An individual might be able to recall the field of strawberries planted next to their primary school when they were six, and the longing with which they used to eye the fruit, but it is almost impossible to remember the state and conditions of being six years old. And it is from these imperfect recollections, as well as the observations we make and the conclusions we draw about the children that surround us, that an idea of childhood emerges, one that is colored by personal experiences, memories, and attitude.

For the purposes of this thesis, childhood will be defined as the time period from birth until twelve years of age, using the onset of puberty to differentiate between childhood and adolescence. This split is based on the differences between biological, psychological and sociological development, as adolescents have already achieved a different level of cognitive ability and are also in the process of gaining independence from the influence of parents and guardians. Furthermore, the construct of Sorin and Galloway's 'agentic child' will serve as a model when it comes to discussing and ana-

---

13 Sorin 13.

14 Natov 2.

lyzing children's books. As stated above, constructs are the only tools with which we can try to map childhood, and the construct of the 'agentic child' is perhaps the most moderate, and the one that would be most appropriate to apply to this time period and society. It assumes, or grants, the child agency in a social setting, sees it as a developing entity, as well as acknowledges childhood as a fluctuating state, while the adult is placed in the position of a guide who helps the child on its journey, and also receives something from the child in return.

2.2. A Maze of Texts: Children's Literature, Problems and Definitions

"Just as most questions imply their answers, so definitions are controlled by their purpose. There can be, therefore, no single definition of 'Children's Literature'," Peter Hunt states in his article "Defining Children's Literature,"[15] thereby highlighting the central problem when attempting to find definitions for this particular field of critical enquiry or genre of literary works. In many ways, the term alone produces a false sense of simplicity, much like the sign heralding the children's section in a bookstore, where a handful of shelves emerge like an island from the sea of 'adult books,' giving the impression of a limited, enclosed space. For children's literature is a complex subject, not easily wrapped into a sentence or two. Subsequently, several issues concerning the classification of children's literature shall be addressed.

2.2.1. Classification Problems

One debated issue is the classification of the field of children's literature. Like a baldachin stretched taut, 'children's literature' encompasses all the text types — drama, novels, short stories, poetry, as well as mixed forms — and genres commonly found in adult literature. This already presents scholars with an extremely large and diverse body of materials to examine. Therefore, it is perhaps slightly misleading to speak of children's literature as a genre, as Tim Wynne-Jones does:

---

15 Hunt 2.

> Genre writing, which includes writing for children, depends upon a recognizable form, however far the envelope is pushed. Writing for adults, on the other hand, by which I mean the books reviewed under the banner of Literature, is, I believe, in this last chapter of the twentieth century, primarily about form. In children's fiction, style is the handmaiden of story, whereas, in adult Literature, story is often the handmaiden of style.[16]

This proposal labels children's literature a 'genre,' which immediately raises a number of questions. For if children's literature is to be considered a genre, would the same apply to adult literature? If not, is children's literature considered to be a genre *of* adult literature, which would mean placing it alongside other genres of adult writing, such as science fiction or satire? Either way, the use of the term 'genre' remains problematic here. Children's literature already encompasses practically all genres also present in adult literature. Thus, in seeing writing for children as a sub-genre of adult literature, one necessarily limits one's possibility of recognizing it in its diversity. Furthermore, since the approach would place children's literature, an umbrella term containing all types of fiction and non-fiction, alongside genres such as science fiction, biography writing, or fantasy, which are characterized by a specific scope, it might call for a re-examination of the term 'genre' altogether. Moreover, there is also the label of 'young adult literature,' which encompasses works of literature written for adolescents of age thirteen and beyond. If one decides to define children's literature as a genre, where is literature for adolescents to be placed? Is it a genre as well, despite the fact that it also includes the same literary genres as adult literature? Is it to be considered a subcategory of children's literature despite the fact that there are significant differences between child and adolescent readers and their assumed need and potential to develop (see chapter 2.1.)? Wynne-Jones' proposal is motivated by the gray areas in literature and fiction: books may be enjoyed by readers of all ages, they may be 'appropriated' by a certain age group (see 2.2.2.), they may even be authored by adolescents or children (2.2.3.).[17] However, this is a dilemma that extends beyond the

---

16 Tim Wynne-Jones, "The Apprehension of Audience: The Difference Between Writing for Adults and Children," *Windows and Words: A Look at Canadian Children's Literature in English*, ed. Aïda Hudson (Ottawa: Ottawa UP, 2003) 14.

17 Aïda Hudson, Introduction, *Windows and Words: A Look at Canadian Children's Literature in English*, ed. Hudson (Ottawa: Ottawa UP, 2003) 3.

field of children's literature. Especially in modernist, postmodernist and other types of 20th- and 21st-century literature, the boundaries between different text types, genres, and audiences become increasingly blurred, until it is difficult to make distinctions. For example, Santos writes about Gertrude Stein's works:

> Stein will always be difficult to categorize, as a perfunctory look at any history of modern American literature will show: is she better discussed under narrative fiction, lyric poetry, drama, or perhaps the theoretical essay? Can one, in Stein, rigorously distinguish one genre from the others? Is *The Geographical History of America* a work of prose or poetry?[18]

This demonstrates that classification problems exist in all areas of literary studies, not merely in children's literature alone. Thus, although Jones' distinctions concerning story-style causality do have merit, labeling children's literature a 'genre' is not likely to resolve the issues that arise from categorizing literature according to age; on the contrary, this attempt creates new, different categorization problems. It is more advisable, especially in the light of 20th-century developments such as the emancipation and increased economic power of adolescents, to use reader age as a distinguishing factor in the classification of literature. This distinction is tied to aspects of physiological and psychological development rather than to the stylistic or formal features of texts, which are more likely to be subject to change over time. Moreover, it does not create the impression of children's and young adult literature as subordinate parts of adult literature, thus allowing to avoid connotations of limited diversity or even of inferiority.

2.2.2. 'Appropriated' Books

Another gray area is formed by the works of fiction which are now considered suitable for children, but which were not originally produced or not primarily produced for a child audience. This includes works such as the collection of folk- and fairytales compiled by the Brothers Grimm and others, Mark Twain's *The Adventures of Huckleberry Finn*, James Fenimore

---

18 Irene Ramalbo Santos, "Gertrude Stein: The Poet as Master of Repetition," *The Cambridge History of American Literature*, ed. Sacvan Bercovitch, Vol. 5 (Cambridge: Cambridge UP, 2003) 208.

Cooper's *The Leatherstocking Tales*, Jonathan Swift's *Gulliver's Travels*,[19] Jules Verne's *20,000 Leagues Under the Sea*, or Charles Dickens' *David Copperfield*. With time, the focal audience of these works of literature shifted, until they eventually came to be considered standard reading material for young audiences. Consider the following excerpt from the film version of *The Neverending Story*:

> COREANDER. The video arcade is down the street. Here we just sell small rectangular objects that are called books. Require a little effort on your part and make no b-b-b-beeps. On your way, please.
>
> BASTIAN. I know books. I have 186 of them at home!
>
> COREANDER. Bah. Comic books.
>
> BASTIAN. No. I've read Treasure Island, Last of the Mohicans, Wizard of Oz, Lord of the Rings, 20,000 Leagues Under the Sea, Tarzan…[20]

In this scene, Bastian, a boy who is described to be about ten or eleven years old[21] in the book version, defends himself against the dismissive attitude of the aging bookseller Coreander by listing his favorite books. Most notably, there is only one book on this list that was written primarily for a child audience, namely *The Wizard of Oz*. The overwhelming majority are works originally written for adult audiences, yet they are nowadays considered suitable for children to such a degree that they have found their way into the dialogue of a popular fantasy movie.

Some works, such as the collections of fairytales, have even been edited over the course of time to appeal more to a young audience. One such example would be the tale of Sleeping Beauty. Originally an oral tale, it was recorded by different writers over time. One of the oldest versions can be found under the name of "Sun, Moon, and Talia" in Giambattista Basile's

---

19 "Children's Literature," *Encyclopædia Britannica*, 2009 ed, Encyclopædia Britannica Online, 15 Oct. 2009 <http://www.britannica.com/EBchecked/topic/111289/childrens-literature>.

20 *The Neverending Story*, dir. Wolfgang Petersen, perf. Noah Hathaway, Barret Oliver, and Tami Stronach, Neue Constantin Film, 1984.

21 Michael Ende, *Die Unendliche Geschichte* (Stuttgart: K. Thienemanns, 1979) 5.

Pentamerone of 1634,[22] which features a young, married king raping Talia (Sleeping Beauty) in her enchanted sleep. Subsequently, the king's wife is overcome with jealousy, orders Talia's children to be killed and served to her husband as a meal. When the entire intrigue finally unravels, the king orders his wife and her co-conspirators to be burned at the stake, in order to be free and marry Talia.[23] In the 1697 version by Charles Perrault, entitled "La Belle au Bois Dormant," the rape of Sleeping Beauty is removed and the young king becomes an unmarried prince — in this version, it is the prince's mother who desires to devour Sleeping Beauty's children, and who eventually dies by throwing herself into a tub filled with venomous snakes.[24] The tale is further edited in *Children and Household Tales*, the 1812 fairytale collection compiled by the Brothers Grimm. Here, the emphasis on a child audience can be detected in the collection's title, and the tale of "Little Briar Rose" ends with Sleeping Beauty waking upon being kissed by the prince, followed by the now famous ending phrase 'and they lived happily ever after.'[25] A similar change can also be observed in many other fairytales, which become progressively less violent and sexually oriented to appear suitable for their progressively younger audience. These examples show, above all, the fluidity of the concept of childhood, but they also present an area of research that is different from the more contemporary works of children's literature, which are written with a focus on audiences up to the age of twelve.

---

22 Linda Hagge, "Pentamerone," *Iowa State University*, 22 Jan. 1999, 4 Dec. 2009 <http://www.public.iastate.edu/~lhagge/newpage6.htm>.

23 Giambattista Basile, "Sonne, Mond, und Talia," *Das Märchen aller Märchen: Der Pentameron,* ed. Walter Boehlich (Frankfurt am Main: Insel, 1982) 45-63.

24 Charles Perrault, "La Belle au Bois Dormant," *Contes*, ed. Marc Soriano (Paris: Flammarion, 1989) 243-253.

25 Jacob Grimm and Wilhelm Grimm, eds., "Dornröschen," *Ausgewählte Kinder- und Hausmärchen* (Stuttgart: Reclam, 1981) 101-106.

2.2.3. Writing by Children

Literature produced by children is also a phenomenon that is difficult to categorize in the literary context, primarily because the field of children's literature is largely maintained and dominated by adult authors who write *for* children, whereas published writing *by* children is treated as a marginal phenomenon. Historically speaking, the publication of texts written by child authors happened a lot less frequently than the publication of adult writings for children. This can be attributed to economic factors such as access to education and leisure time,[26] but also to the lack of a forum traditionally made available to child authors in the world of literary publishing. Yet child and adolescent writers are nowhere near as rare as one would perhaps think. According to Alexander and McMaster, "for centuries children have been taking the pen into their hands, and writing (as David Copperfield says of his childhood reading) 'as if for life'."[27] Beginning with the early 19th and ending with the first half of the 20th century, the examples listed in the book are numerous — Lord Byron, Jane Austen, the Brontë siblings, George Eliot, Elizabeth Barrett Browning, Lewis Carroll and Virginia Woolf all began to write at a very young age,[28] although it should be noted here that Alexander and McMaster do not distinguish between child and adolescent writing — juvenilia produced by the adolescent Jane Austen are examined side by side with publications written by children under the age of twelve, such as Daisy Ashford and Marjory Fleming. The increasing evidence of child and adolescent writers in the 19th century can be attributed to a variety of reasons. Firstly, as mentioned previously in chapter 2.1., the formation of a sufficiently wealthy middle and upper class in the wake of the Industrial Revolution increased educational possibilities for children. Secondly, the literary climate of the period made both reading at home and family reading fashionable, thereby introducing children to a

---

26 Christine Alexander, "Nineteenth-century Juvenilia: A Survey," *The Child Writer from Austen to Woolf*, eds. Christine Alexander and Juliet McMaster (Cambridge: Cambridge UP, 2005) 11.

27 Christine Alexander and Juliet McMaster, Introduction, *The Child Writer from Austen to Woolf*, eds. Alexander and McMaster (Cambridge: Cambridge UP, 2005) 1.

28 Alexander, "Nineteenth-century Juvenilia" 11.

large variety of literary works and magazines, some of which, such as Our Young Folks or St Nicholas Magazine, even sought contributions from children.[29] Thirdly, the Romantic movement, which idealized childhood, and the discoveries of the 19th century, which included the publication of Charles Darwin's theory of evolution, radically changed Victorian society. As a result, many writers turned to the idea of the child and the process of growing up to explore their own origins and their place in the world.[30] This new consciousness of childhood, in turn, fuelled the desire to see writings by increasingly younger authors.

The reasons why children and young adults take up the pen are as varied and numerous as the reasons of adult writers; however, child writers tend to fight a losing battle for authenticity once their works are discovered and published. Although professionally published books generally undergo an extensive editing process, the child writer is supervised and controlled in ways most adult writers are not. They are not simply restricted by their editors' preferences, but also by their editors' conceptions of childhood and what is 'appropriate writing' for a child author. This was the case with Marjory Fleming's writings, who was born in Scotland in 1803, and who unintentionally became an iconic figure through her writings in the middle of the 19th century. Encouraged from an early age to practice her handwriting, Fleming began to record her experiences in a notebook, until she died of an illness at the age of eight. More than fifty years later, her writings were discovered by H. B. Farnie, a journalist, who used her notebook to create the sensationalist story of "Pet Marjorie."[31] This was picked up five years later by Dr. John Brown, who heavily edited Fleming's original work to suit the Victorian idea of the child writer, citing her friendship with the famed poet Sir Walter Scott to gain further publicity:

29 Alexander, "Nineteenth-century Juvenilia" 20-21.

30 Alexander, "Nineteenth-century Juvenilia" 26.

31 Alexander, "Nineteenth-century Juvenilia" 14.

> Sir Walter was in that house almost every day, and had a key, so in he and the hound went, shaking themselves in the lobby. 'Marjorie! Marjorie!' shouted her friend, 'where are ye, my bonnie wee croodlin doo?' In a moment a bright, eager child of seven was in his arms, and he was kissing her all over.[32]

This story later proved to be fabricated, but the embellished, sentimental tale of the "rosy little wifie"[33] still took the public imagination by storm.[34] A partially comparable fate befell Anne Frank's diary, recording her experiences as she and her family hid from prosecution by the Nazi regime in the years 1942-1944. The diary was posthumously published by her father, who decided to edit her writings for sexual content and unfavorable commentary on her family and their companions, since openly sexual discourse in young adult books was not considered proper in post-war Europe.[35] Both examples show how much of the child writer is controlled by the adult world — adult notions of childhood and propriety heavily influence the authenticity of works written by children and adolescents, denying them aspects of themselves such as outbursts of temper, sexual thoughts and feelings, or, as in the case of Marjory Fleming, even an authentic biography.

Another point of interest is that writings by children tend to come under suspicion of fraud. It appears as if to many, it is inconceivable that a child could craft imaginative, challenging works that also capture the attention of adults, and thus, thoughts tend to turn towards dishonesty first of all. This happened to the novel *The Young Visiters: Or, Mr. Salteena's Plan*, a story about upper-class intrigue written by the nine-year-old Daisy Ashford, which was published in Britain in 1919, or the poetry works by ten-year-old Nathalia Crane, published in 1924 under the title *Janitor's Boy and Other Poems*. The 'unchildlike' writing inspired controversy and debate — Ashford's book was ascribed to J. M. Barrie, who had written the preface for its publication, and comparable accusations were made against Crane's

---

32 John Brown, *Pet Marjorie: A Story of Child-Life Fifty Years Ago* (Edinburgh: William P. Nimmo, 1864), *GoogleBooks*, 11 Dec. 2009 <http://books.google.ca/>.

33 Brown 26.

34 Alexander, "Nineteenth-century Juvenilia" 14.

35 Mirjam Pressler, ed. *Anne Frank Tagebuch* (Frankfurt am Main: Fischer, 1998) 5-6.

work.[36] Contemporary American child novelist Nancy Yi Fan, who started writing *Swordbird*, her first fantasy novel, at the age of ten, met with similar problems long before she attempted to get published, when her school teacher refused to believe that her short stories were indeed authored by her, and summoned her father to ensure that he was not writing them in her stead.[37] Of course, writing talent rarely flourishes without guidance. When one examines the lives of child writers, many are found to have extensive access to literature as part of their education, and are often encouraged by family members or guardians to pursue writing as an activity. Such is the case with the Brontë siblings, who liked to read the Blackwood's Edinburgh Magazine's philosophical articles and literary publications and found themselves inspired to create their own fictional worlds;[38] such is the case with Virginia Woolf, whose work was influenced by the storytelling, reading and writing practices of her family,[39] and such is the case with contemporary young writers like Fan, whose parents exposed her to a wide variety of art and literature from a very early age,[40] or Christopher Paolini, whose young adult fantasy novel *Eragon* was edited and published by his family members.[41] However, it is curious to see how often these feats are diminished in the eyes of the adult world, not examined for what they are but taken as signs of the great things to come. "Lip service is paid to juvenile works in most literary or historical biographies; early writings are often seen as portents of greatness but are quickly dismissed as immature, derivative, or fragmented works,"[42] Christine Alexander writes, pointing out how

---

36 Ann Hulbert, "Wordbound: Child Writers Break Into Print," *Slate,* 12 July 2004, 11 Dec. 2009 <http://www.slate.com/id/2103752/>.

37 Lucie Young. "Flight of Fantasy." *Telegraph.co.uk*, 27 Jan. 2007, 11 Dec. 2009 <http://www.telegraph.co.uk/culture/3662784/Flight-of-fantasy.html>.

38 Christine Alexander. "Play and Apprenticeship: The Culture of Family Magazines." *The Child Writer from Austen to Woolf*, eds. Christine Alexander and Juliet McMaster (Cambridge: Cambridge UP, 2005) 34.

39 Alexander, "Play and Apprenticeship" 42.

40 Young, "Flight of Fancy."

41 Hulbert, "Wordbound."

42 Christine Alexander, "Autobiography and Juvenilia: The Fractured Self in Charlotte Brontë's Early Manuscripts," *The Child Writer from Austen to Woolf,* eds. Christine Alexander and Juliet McMaster (Cambridge: Cambridge UP, 2005) 154.

once again, the child is seen as subordinate to the adult, incomplete and 'just not quite as good.'

The above points serve to illustrate some of the difficulties in approaching the complex field of children's literature. Due to the social circumstances surrounding the production and reception of literature in general, as well as the modern concept of childhood, which only began to emerge towards the 19th century, children's literature is relatively young, but has quickly evolved into a field that is as multifaceted as adult literature. However, it is precisely because of its ever-increasing diversity and influence that it is important to remain aware of the mechanics behind the creation and dissemination of children's books. To a large degree, everything to do with their production process — the authors, the content, the printing, and consequently the availability of children's books — are subject to, if not adult control, then at least adult scrutiny, which is largely swayed by the constructs of childhood ingrained in the individual adult and the collective adult society's mind. Although this kind of control is not to be viewed as a negative factor by default, it can also easily come to deny children the abilities they possess and dictate the rules and content of books primarily aimed at children, which will be discussed in detail in the following chapter. Moreover, for the purposes of this thesis, it should be noted that the subsequent use of the terms "children's books" and "children's literature" will refer to a particular type of writing produced in this vast field — namely books aimed primarily at a child audience, produced by adult writers, since the discussion of appropriated children's books and child authors would go far beyond the scope of this paper.

2.3. Reading over Shoulders: The Implicit Adult Audience

Having covered the adult influence, past and present, on the production of children's books, this chapter will turn to another characteristic of children's books that is easily overlooked, namely its dual readership. Although, by its modern definition, children's literature is aimed at children, they are not its exclusive audience. Behind a child reader, there tends to be an adult reader, and thus, children's books are also designed to appeal to adults. The major difference between children's books and other areas of literature is that in no other field is there such a power difference between two groups of readers. Contrary to other types of literature, which may be mainly aimed at one particular audience but can also be accessed and enjoyed by another, children's literature *has* to appeal to the adult reader. One might go so far as to say that children only read children's literature by proxy, for it is the adult who decides on its value, appeal, and chooses to buy it for the child after it has been judged satisfactory. Shavit points out that the phenomenon of parental control has only become manifest in the past few decades, stating that never before has "the notion of childhood been as dominant as it is today, nor has the presence of the child in Western culture been so striking."[43] Moreover, with this increasing emphasis on the child and its well-being in Western society, children's literature has come to fulfill certain functions that go beyond the earlier notions of reading for intellectual and spiritual education — it is now supposed to help the child in general, to cater to its emotional and psychological needs, and is thus required to meet certain adult expectations.[44] Partly, adult involvement in the selection and reading of children's literature is a natural phenomenon, as Hans-Heino Ewers explains:

> Literarische Aktionsfähigkeit ist nicht die Voraussetzung, sondern das Resultat des kinderliterarischen Kommunikationsprozesses. Die Mitwirkung des Erwach-

---

43 Zohar Shavit, "The Double Attribution of Texts for Children and How it Affects Writing for Children," *Transcending Boundaries: Writing for a Dual Audience of Children and Adults*, ed. Sandra L. Beckett (New York: Garland, 1999) 85.

44 Shavit 86.

> senen an ihm ist deshalb, so meine ich, nicht per se ein Akt der Bevormundung; ohne sie käme die kinderliterarische Kommunikation schwerlich in Gang.[45]

Although the adult is not automatically domineering or patronizing, they can easily adopt such an attitude since it is difficult for adults to distinguish when their assistance and guidance is necessary and when they begin to dictate children's preferences and capabilities — for the older children become, the more adult interference becomes an act of patronization.[46] Since adults, whether patronizing or not, are very much involved in children's literature, the author of a children's book is required to seek adult approval or run the risk of not reaching their intended audience at all. The presence of the adult reader, who is also its critic, is responsible for certain trends in children's literature that both restrict and liberate it. For example, Ewers states, the adult reader is more likely to focus on the pedagogical value of a children's text and will thus be more inclined to demand an affirmation of meaningful qualities rather than full disclosure or disillusionment commonly found in adult fiction. This restrictiveness is countered by the adult's willingness to accept what they would see as outdated styles of composition in other fields, allowing children's literature greater freedom to experiment with style and form.[47]

The adult addressee also leaves their traces in traditional features such as prefaces and epilogues, designed to explain textual background or give advice when reading the book to children. For instance, this is the case in David Bouchard's *The Dragon New Year: A Chinese Legend* or Andrea Spalding's *Solomon's Tree* — Bouchard uses an epilogue to elaborate on the historical background of Buddha and the traditional Chinese Dragon Dance,

---

45 Hans-Heino Ewers, "Das doppelsinnige Kinderbuch: Erwachsene als Mitleser und als Leser von Kinderliteratur," *Kinderliteratur — Literatur auch für Erwachsene?* ed. Dagmar Grenz (München: Fink, 1990) 15. "The ability to make choices concerning literature is not the prerequisite, but the result of the communicative process of children's literature. The participation of the adult — to my mind — is therefore not an act of patronization per se. Without it, communication on children's literature would hardly get under way." (own trans.)

46 Ewers 15-16.

47 Ewers 16-17.

both of which feature in the story,[48] as does Spalding in order to explain the carving of masks and mythological figures of Tsimshian culture.[49] Although appendices can be informative for the child reader, what they primarily address is the adult, who is seeking reassurance that the book will satisfy their demand for accuracy. Another feature born of awareness of the adult reader is the inclusion of the adult in the reading process. This inclusion can take place in a number of ways — one prominent possibility is the formation of different 'levels' through symbolism, irony and ambiguity, as is the case in Lewis Carroll's *Alice's Adventures in Wonderland*. Here, the text allows for different readings, appealing to a dual readership with at times very different capabilities and interests, and capturing the attention and imagination of both. Other possibilities are wordplay and "nudges" directed at an obviously older audience — for example, Scott cites a picturebook by Colin Thompson called *Looking for Atlantis*, which features numerous puns on adult classics such as *Finnegan's Wake* (called 'Finnegan's Whale' in Thompson's work) or *Moll Flanders* ('Moll Flounders'), along with linguistic play involving foreign languages.[50] Opinions differ wildly on whether these layers of meaning and language play belong in a children's book or not. According to the writer C. S. Lewis, "a children's story which is enjoyed only by children is a bad children's story,"[51] which is counterpoint to Shavit's view that this type of writing is in danger of ignoring the child reader in favor of catering to the adult who is reading along.[52] Yet, there is no reason why the writing of children's literature should be an exclusive act. There are children's books which pay very little attention to actively including the adult in the narrative, books which, as Ewers puts it, are supposed to be to children as toys, playful and engaging without the

48 David Bouchard, *The Dragon New Year: A Chinese Legend* (Vancouver: Raincoast, 1999) 28-29.

49 Andrea Spalding, *Solomon's Tree* (Victoria: Orca, 2002) 30.

50 Carole Scott, "Dual Audience in Picturebooks,' *Transcending Boundaries: Writing for a Dual Audience of Children and Adults*, ed. Sandra L. Beckett (New York: Garland, 1999) 102.

51 C.S. Lewis, qtd. in Shavit 87.

52 Shavit 90.

interference of adults.[53] Seeing the catering to adults as a textual requirement diminishes the creative freedom of children's writers. Conversely, the same can be said for the near-total exclusion of the adult reader. There is nothing wrong with addressing multiple audiences in a children's book, however, the writer has to be dedicated to keeping the balance in this balancing act. As long as the child's emotional and intellectual enjoyment of a story are not diminished, puns directed at adult readers may serve as points of communication between the child and the adult — something that is even more readily apparent when one considers picturebooks in particular, which invite discussion about the visual aspects as well as the text. And for another, such narrative levels may also contribute to the longevity of a children's book — by not simply invoking the nostalgia of the adult reader's "inner child," but by allowing the child to discover new aspects to a story as it grows and gains experience.

2.4. The Silent Child: Child Readers, Their Abilities and Perceptions

Much of the discussion thus far has centered on the role of the adult in children's literature — its production, dissemination, reception, and judgment. However, this would mean omitting the consideration of the primary audience, namely the children, and how they respond to books. This particular field of study is relatively young, emerging only in the late 1970s, mainly due to the scholarly prejudices against both children's books, which were not perceived as literature, and children themselves, who were not thought to have sufficient experience and capabilities to respond.[54] And yet, children do respond, sometimes profoundly, to the texts they read. Although their life experience may be limited by the comparatively small number of years they have spent in this world, they are capable of questioning, analyzing, and connecting the material they consume, whether by reading or being read to, and of honing these skills over time. Sipe categorizes children's responses to literature according to author, text, reader and con-

53 Ewers 17.

54 Barbara D. Stoodt-Hill and Linda B. Amspaugh-Corson. *Children's Literature: Discovery of a Lifetime* (Melbourne: Macmillan, 1996) 82.

text.[55] According to Sipe, children freely question an author's or illustrator's intent — why texts develop the way they do, or why pictures contain certain objects or colors.[56] This coincides with Nodelman's observations about children's ability to take in and decipher pictures by devoting the same attention to all their details, not merely their focal aspects.[57] In terms of text, children may make connections to other books they have read, or link what is happening in the story to their own personal experiences. They tend to draw on all parts of a book — its cover, title page, illustrations, and dedications — to derive meaning from it.[58] In a 1991 study conducted among kindergarten, second- and fourth-grade children, Lehr found that even kindergarten children are already capable of certain levels of textual abstraction, by being able to summarize and identify themes in stories, as well as cross-reference stories with similar themes, although this is more likely to occur in realistic fiction than fantastic and more symbolic folk tales.[59] Concerning reader response, Sipe points out that children's reactions can vary greatly, as they may embrace aspects of a text due to identifying with characters on a personal level, or they may resist what is being presented to them, such as events and behavior to which they object.[60] Moreover, children tend to respond to stories more freely than adults, for example by playfully reenacting what they are told. Wells Rowe's study focusing both on children in classroom situations and her own young son's reactions at home presents comprehensive data on different types of dramatic play, and, more importantly, the attention to detail that children exhibit in their games. For instance, Wells Rowe observes her son's careful selection of toys and props,

---

55 Lawrence R Sipe, "Children's Response to Literature: Author, Text, Reader, Context," *Theory into Practice* 38.3 (Summer 1999) 120.

56 Sipe 121.

57 Perry Nodelman, "How Picture Books Work," *Understanding Children's Literature,* ed. Peter Hunt, 2nd ed. (New York: Routledge, 2005) 132.

58 Sipe 122.

59 Susan S. Lehr, "The Child's Developing Sense of Theme as a Response to Literature," *Reading Research Quarterly* 23.3 (Summer 1988) 337.

60 Sipe 123.

and the increasing complexity of his reenactment over time,[61] but also the fact that children, when discussing or answering questions about a story, tend to play-act freely — sometimes answering as themselves, sometimes replying in the role of a specific character from the book.[62] Moreover, children also respond differently to literature in certain contexts. Sipe cites the example of a classroom situation where children were encouraged to speak up during the reading-aloud of a story, which greatly facilitated literary communication, and notes that responses will vary depending on what is considered acceptable in which context; that is, how freely children are allowed to respond — by bringing toys, moving about, or fetching books they perceive as relevant or related to the story being read.[63] Naturally, the cultural background or the influence of extra-literary sources such as the vast field of popular culture may also play a role in the way children react to the books they read. Sipe demonstrates the latter by citing the example of a first- or second-grade child who used her knowledge of a television series to make a highly symbolic observation during the reading of Bunting's *Fly Away Home*, a story about a homeless boy whose mother has died, and who lives with his father at the airport. In the story, the boy finds a trapped bird, which later escapes through a temporary gap in a door. One of the pupils listening to the story perceived the bird to be the spirit of the boy's mother, by drawing on her knowledge of the television show *Married With Children*, which features a talking dog.[64] (It should be noted here that Sipe describes the dog as a character who "had been transformed into a dog."[65] However, the dog is supposed to be merely a canine with a human voice-over, not an enchanted human. In addition to that, the show features an episode in which the dog dies and is subsequently reincarnated. This might have facilitated the child's idea concerning the mother/bird spirit me-

---

61 Deborah Wells Rowe, "The Literate Potentials of Book-Related Dramatic Play," *Reading Research Quarterly* 33.1 (Jan-Feb-Mar. 1998) 18.

62 Rowe 22.

63 Sipe 125.

64 Sipe 127.

65 Sipe 127.

taphor).[66] The above-mentioned and many other, similar studies show children's varied ways of response, and also demonstrate their ability to understand, process, and question the material they read. In some ways, they examine books more holistically than adults by including all parts of the book, not simply the text and illustrations therein. Far from being passive consumers who are "fed" books by adults, they tend to show a keen ability to connect with and dissect books on both a textual and a visual level.

2.5. Picture Books and Picturebooks

Almost four centuries have passed since John Amos Comenius' publication of the *Orbis Sensualium Pictus* in 1658, which is considered to be the first illustrated work for children. Since then, just as children's literature in general has expanded beyond the realm of education, so have illustrated works for children left the realm of the purely educational to explore many different possibilities and purposes. Hence, when one speaks of "picture books" now, one has to take a closer look at the ambiguity of the term. It is used to denote a number of different types of books, all of which heavily feature illustrated material. It should be noted that this chapter will focus solely on picture books designed for children; illustrated works for adults, photography books, and comics will not be considered, as discussing all of them would go far beyond the scope of this paper. One of the first types of children's picture books that comes to mind is the picture book for infants and pre-literate ages, often made of cardboard or otherwise sturdy material to withstand accidental tearing and to reduce the danger of injuries via paper cuts. This kind of book features very little text, if any, as it is mainly based around enhancing recognition skills of small children.[67] Another type of picture book is the toy book, which takes illustrations into the three-dimensional realm by using fold-out pages, pop-up elements, visual riddles, movable parts and layer concepts to engage children on an interactive level, something that has led critics like Saltman to refer to them as "semi-

---

66 "Married With Children: Requiem for a Dead Briard," *IMDb*, 2009, The Internet Movie Database, 11 Dec. 2009 <http://www.imdb.com/title/tt0642359>.

67 Judith Saltman, *Modern Canadian Children's Books* (Toronto: Oxford UP, 1987) 30.

books."[68] The concept book is another type of illustrated book, which Carlson defines as "a book intended for young children (i.e., under 5) that focuses on colors, shapes, sizes, number and counting, and the alphabet,"[69] in other words, a type of book that focuses on developing young children's identification and grouping skills. Illustrated books may also find application in the realm of language learning, in the form of mono-, bi- or multilingual publications of varying difficulty stages and structure, which are designed to help with the acquisition of vocabulary and grammar.[70] However, this thesis will focus on yet another type of picture book, one whose primary purpose is not to be instructive, but whose primary concern is to tell a story in combination with images. Up until this point, this type has been referred to via the compound spelling "picturebook," and will continue to do so, thereby following the suggestion of Driggs Wolfenbarger and Sipe, who argue that this compound is best suited to represent the idea of the union between image and text, because "a picturebook is not simply a book that happens to have pictures."[71]

Among the many different forms and modes of storytelling, the picturebook stands out. Its stories expand into two dimensions, art and literature, two spheres which communicate concepts in very different ways. Contrary to entirely written publications, the picturebook is charged with the difficult task of uniting these two spheres into a single whole, a whole that is more than the sum of its parts. As with any collaboration, the picturebook requires certain concessions on the part of these two mediums. Both limit the other as well as expand its meaning and impact. One such important constraint would be brevity. Since the text is supported by images, the written narrative no longer requires the same amount of descriptiveness and words that would be necessary to create a story without pictures. Yet the picturebook authors are required to find a concise, distilled language to convey

---

68 Saltman, *Modern Canadian Children's Books* 30.

69 Ann D. Carlson, "Concept Books and Young Children," *Ways of Knowing*, 1996, Rutgers School of Communication and Information, 11 Dec. 2009 <http://comminfo.rutgers.edu/professional-development/childlit/books/CARLSON.pdf>.

70 Saltman, *Modern Canadian Children's Books* 38-39.

71 Carol Driggs Wolfenbarger, and Lawrence Sipe, "A Unique Visual and Literary Art Form: Recent Research on Picturebooks," *Language Arts* 83.3 (2007): 273.

thoughts and feelings. Lunn points out that this is especially important for younger audiences, whose reading and text comprehension skills are still developing.[72] Another constraint is complementariness. Nikolajeva and Scott define five ways in which text and pictures might interact in picturebooks: Their relationship can be one of symmetry, each providing the same content as the other. It can be complementary, both providing related information which is similar, but not the same, or text and image might enhance each other's meaning. Apart from this, they may also have a counterpoint or even contradictory relationship, telling different stories altogether.[73] However, Driggs Wolfenbarger and Sipe point out that readers generally expect the illustrations and the text to match to a certain degree, at least thematically, and may be perplexed upon finding this expectation not fulfilled.[74] Especially young children require a degree of thematic cohesion and complementariness in picturebooks, as depending on their age, their capabilities for abstract thought and analysis are still developing. However, this does not mean that the text and images have to match completely. A picture may show a broader aspect of what is written in the text, or may focus on a smaller detail. It is in the subtle differences between text and image, the interplay, that will delight readers the most.[75] Moreover, Saltman states that there is a certain inequality in the way the image and the word grab the reader's attention — the visual image has a certain edge over the text, since humans are visual beings who are more likely to be drawn to the concreteness of an image than the relative abstractness of a written text.[76]

And yet, comparatively little heed is paid to book illustrations, both by readers in general and scholars in particular. According to Nodelman, they are taken for granted and are summarily dismissed as simple, when in actuality, images transport a wealth of messages that speak not just to the read-

---

72 Janet Lunn, "The Picture Book: A Commentary," *Windows and Words: A Look at Canadian Children's Literature in English*, eds. Aida Hudson and Susan-Ann Cooper (Ottawa: Ottawa UP, 2003) 185.

73 Nikolajeva and Scott, qtd. in Driggs Wolfenbarger and Sipe 274.

74 Driggs Wolfenbarger and Sipe 273.

75 Driggs Wolfenbarger and Sipe 274.

76 Saltman, *Modern Canadian Children's Books* 19.

er's conscious, but also their subconscious.[77] This attitude may at least in part be inspired by the literary prejudice of Western society, which elevates the written text over the image, and sees illustrations, if not as a threat to culture and intellectuality, then at least as not worth thinking about.[78] Yet illustrations convey a multitude of things in ways that extend beyond the accompanying text. The way the characters dress, their stance, their facial expressions, the focus of the image, and many other aspects, communicate social norms, values, and features of a culture both implicitly and explicitly. Thus, picturebooks become transporters, or agents, of the culture that produces them. In addition to that, the primary audience of children's picturebooks are the young and inexperienced, those who are, as Nodelman puts it, "[...] in need of learning how to think about their world, how to see and understand themselves and others. Consequently, picture books are a significant means by which we integrate young children into the ideology of our culture."[79] For these reasons, the subsequent analysis of selected children's picturebooks in chapters 4 and 5 will focus on both the meaning expressed by the text and the meaning expressed by the respective illustrations in order to allow for a more detailed impression of the themes presented therein.

77 Nodelman 131.

78 Gunther R. Kress, and Theo van Leeuwen, *Reading Images: The Grammar of Visual Design* (New York: Routledge, 1996) 16-17.

79 Nodelman 131.

3. Towards Canada

Having outlined the necessary premise for a discourse on children's literature, the following section will turn towards the development and role of children's literature, and, more specifically, children's picturebooks in Canada. Long confined to a marginal role due to the country's colonial history, children's literature in Canada has evolved explosively during the last four decades, becoming one of the fastest growing segments of the literary market. Picturebooks, formerly lackluster productions subject to the constraints of technology and the spirit of the times, have become varied, colorful gems that delight children and adults alike. And, most importantly, these new picturebooks have begun to reach out to all segments of the Canadian population with a large amount of special interest topics such as problem narratives, green narratives, or narratives with the aim of preserving and promoting certain cultural aspects. Many of the contemporary regional and ethnocultural picturebooks are a response to the current climate in Canada, a country wherein very different cultural groups live together to form a mosaic society, whose pieces might not always click into place without difficulty. The subsequent points will attempt to explore the developments leading up to the current status of children's books in Canada and focus on the role of the ethnocultural and regional narratives in particular.

3.1. Canadian Children's Literature

What makes Canadian children's literature Canadian? When attempting to define "Canadianness," one is looking for markers or issues that have shaped a particular national identity — recurring themes that, in ever-changing guises, trouble or preoccupy the citizens of a country and are reflected in writing. There is some dispute concerning the start of Canadian literature for children, as critics approach the issue from two different viewpoints. Some, like Elizabeth Waterston, give consideration to all works for children published in Canada over time, while some, like Roderick McGillis, tie the beginning of Canadian children's literature to the surfacing of a uniquely Canadian consciousness, a national identity not tied to its French and British colonizers.[80] McGillis' distinction is based on the sudden, sharp increase in publications for children after 1975, something that other critics have also remarked on. "Many publishers, writers, and critics have observed that our children's literature may go back over 100 years, but that it has only shown significant growth in the last twenty-five to thirty years,"[81] Judith Saltman remarks at the beginning of her résumé "Canadian Children's Literature at the Millennium," while McGillis cites a rather caustic statement by Northrop Frye, who "remarked that any criticism of Canadian literature based on evaluative principles 'would become only a debunking project,' leaving this literature a 'poor naked *alouette* plucked of every feather of decency and dignity'."[82] McGillis attributes this increase in publications to several important events which took place in the 1960s and 1970s, such as the centennial celebration of the anniversary of the British North America Act (informally known as Canada Day) in 1967, the acquisition of its own flag, as well as the Summit Series of hockey games against the USSR in 1972, which raised Canada's self-awareness and confidence as a nation.[83]

The publications for children in the early period of settlement are limited to regional catechisms and prayer books,[84] as it took a long time to establish a more widespread publishing industry. The first works of Canadian children's fiction in the mid-19th century mainly focus on the harsh and impenetrable wilderness of the North, frontier life, and survival.[85] In fact, Margaret Atwood identifies survival and its central character archetype, the victim, as the theme in many works of Canadian literature, no matter where and when they are written — whether it is the first settlers' fight against the

---

80 Roderick McGillis, "Canada," *Children's Literature: An Illustrated History,* ed. Peter Hunt (Oxford: Oxford UP, 1995) 334.

81 Judith Saltman, "Canadian Children's Literature at the Millennium," *Windows and Words: A Look at Canadian Children's Literature in English*, eds. Aïda Hudson and Susan-Ann Cooper (Ottawa: Ottawa UP, 2003) 23.

82 McGillis 333.

83 McGillis 334.

84 Elizabeth Waterston, *Children's Literature in Canada* (New York: Twayne, 1992) 2.

85 Saltman, "Canadian Children's Literature at the Millennium" 23.

hostile conditions in the new country, the French Canadian feelings of marginalization, or the English Canadian fear of increasing Americanization.[86] Waterston identifies a sense of this struggle in Canadian children's books, as well, noting that the survival mentality has contributed to a heightened Canadian awareness towards minorities and victimized groups.[87] Moreover, she notes the emergence of themes such as humor, honesty, kindness and the will to work hard in characters of 20th-century children's narratives, remarking that Canadians have come to see these qualities as national values.[88] And these qualities are certainly beneficial to contemporary Canadian society and its children's literature. With one of the world's highest immigration rates per capita,[89] Canada has become a multicultural nation in the sense that many different cultures congregate within its boundaries. In the age of multiculturalism and globalization, it is more difficult than ever to define Canadian children's literature, to draw boundaries and distinctions. Criteria such as the place of the author's residence, place of birth, his or her ethnicity, or his or her chosen language can no longer be used to identify what is Canadian writing, if, indeed, these criteria ever could be used at all. Is the children's book written by the English Canadian author living in Australia a Canadian children's book? What about the Chinese Canadian author who was born in China, yet has immigrated to Canada and continues to live and publish there? What about children's books published in Canada in languages other than French or English? What about books that are published simultaneously in Canada and the US? Whichever parameters one chooses, one is invariably going to struggle with exceptions on top of exceptions, an insoluble categorization dilemma. Thus, it is perhaps best to approach the subject from a different perspective and propose that Canadian children's literature is everything that defines itself as such.

---

86 Margaret Atwood, *Survival: A Thematic Guide to Canadian Literature* (Toronto: Anansi, 1972) 32.

87 Waterston 3.

88 Waterston 4.

89 *Statistics Canada, Population by Selected Ethnic Origins, by Province and Territory* (2006 Census), 20 Nov. 2009, 11 Dec. 2009 <http://www40.statcan.gc.ca/l01/cst01/demo26a-eng.htm>.

3.2. Development of Canadian Children's Picturebooks

In the Canadian context, picturebooks occupy a special position among other literary publications aimed at children. As mentioned in the previous chapter, Canadian children's literature only began to expand in the last four decades due to Canada's historical situation and the slow emergence of a distinctly Canadian consciousness. Picturebooks, however, did particularly suffer from lack of representation *and* presentation. Until the 1970s, what little material was published was usually impaired by the technological limitations of the time — the printing of aesthetically pleasing, multicolored picturebooks was extremely complex and expensive, thus the production of picturebooks was largely neglected, and publications were generally "poorly produced, limited to black and white or monochromatic illustrations, and uninspired in design, execution, and theme."[90] Yet with the new enthusiasm for children's literature inspired by the wave of nationalism in the 1970s, picturebooks rose to become one of the most important and fastest-growing segments of children's literature.[91] Naturally, the technological advancements of the information era also contributed to the sudden increase in diversity and production rates. A quote from typographer and layout designer Michael Solomon perhaps best highlights these immense leaps in technological (and digital) possibilities:

> Once I have received an edited picture book manuscript (usually now already captured on diskette in a word-processing program), I create a complete page layout on the computer with many determinations, such as the editor's (sometimes my) page breaks, fonts, sizes, measure, leading, and the grid (comprising text and picture column placement, margins, and bleeds) made but not 'carved in stone.' For this layout is then sent to the illustrator, with the overriding proviso that all of this, though professional and final-looking, should be treated only as a starting point.[92]

This case shows how far layout possibilities alone have advanced since the 1970s, an example that can be expanded to include the entire printing and

90 Saltman, *Modern Canadian Children's Books* 19.

91 Saltman, *Modern Canadian Children's Books* 19.

92 Michael Solomon, "Publishing Children's Picture Books: The Role of Design and Art Direction," *Windows and Words: A Look at Canadian Children's Literature in English*, eds. Aïda Hudson and Susan-Ann Cooper (Ottawa: Ottawa UP, 2003) 194.

publishing industry. The advent of desktop publishing with the introduction of personal computers, the invention of faster and cheaper printing and copying methods, and the development of digital design have opened up new modes of artistic expression and new possibilities for presentation, allowing for the printing of picturebooks which were simply impossible to create before the beginning of the PC-era in the 1970s, or whose production was at least extremely difficult and costly. Saltman cites two factors beyond the social and technological factors which influenced the growth of picturebook publications. One is the relocation of a majority of the printing industry to Hong Kong,[93] which allowed for cheaper color printing, a development that can still be observed in picturebooks even today — from the works selected for discussion in this thesis, four out of ten books were printed in Hong Kong, and three more were printed in China or Singapore. Solomon also remarks on the constant struggle between printing costs and the wish to produce artistic, challenging books, stating that all-too extravagant printing caprice is usually avoided. In the event that techniques like foil stamping, fluorescent inks and other effects are used, it is never out of pure fancy.[94] Another reason is the pioneer work of several picturebook authors and illustrators who explored new methods of art, expression, format and style,[95] such as the joint efforts of illustrator Elizabeth Cleaver and author William Toye, whose works were among the first fully colored Canadian picturebooks for children.[96]

Nowadays, children's books in general and picturebooks in particular enjoy widespread popularity and attention in Canada. The Canadian Children's Book Center (CCBC), founded in 1976, has become one of the most influential organizations dedicated to the promotion and support of reading, writing, and illustration of Canadian children's books, offering advice and

93 Saltman, *Modern Canadian Children's Books* 19.

94 Solomon 199.

95 Saltman, *Modern Canadian Children's Books* 19.

96 Gail Edwards, and Judith Saltman, "Looking at Ourselves, Looking at Others: Multiculturalism in Canadian Children's Picture Books in English." Paper Presented to the History of the Book in Canada's Open Conference for Vol. III. Nov. 2001. 11 Dec. 2009 <http://www.hbic.library.utoronto.ca/vol3edwardssaltman_en.htm>.

assistance to authors and artists seeking publication, connecting with publishers and booksellers across the country, as well as compiling resources for parents and educators.[97] Over a hundred authors and illustrators have chosen to be listed in the directory on the CCBC website as available for visits and readings at schools and libraries across the country.[98] The Canadian Children's Book Week, a CCBC initiative started in 1977 with a modest eleven authors to promote reading and writing of children's books, has morphed into a week-long national event, allowing children across the country to meet with the creators of their favorite books.[99] Moreover, the TD Grade One Book Giveaway, another CCBC project, has been promoting literacy since 2000 by giving every first-grade student a Canadian children's book — usually a picturebook — and, in this manner, providing more than half a million books to children all across Canada for free.[100] The Family Literacy Day, celebrated each year on January 27, was developed by the ABC Canada Literacy Foundation in 1999 in order to encourage families to read together. Recently, the organization hosted an event to set a new world record for simultaneous reading to and with children. Although no new world record was achieved, over 119,000 Canadian families participated on January 23 and 24, 2009.[101] These organizations and festivals show, more than anything, how important children's literature and children's picturebooks have become to the Canadian public, growing into a new form of national entertainment.

---

97 The Canadian Children's Book Center, 2009, CBC, 11 Dec. 2009 <http://www.bookcentre.ca>.

98 The Canadian Children's Book Center.

99 Carol-Ann Hoyte, "Book Week Past and Present," *Bookweek.ca*, 2007, TD Canadian Children's Book Week, 11 Dec. 2009 <http://www.bookweek.ca/history>.

100 "TD Grade One Book Giveaway," *Bookweek.ca*, 2009, Canadian Children's Book Week, 11 Dec. 2009 <http://www.bookweek.ca/book-week/td-grade-one-book-giveaway>.

101 "Family Literacy Day World Record Attempt," *ABC Canada*, 2009, ABC Canada Literacy Foundation, 11 Dec. 2009 <http://www.abc-canada.org/fldworldrecord>.

3.3. Multiculturalism

While picturebooks previously dealt with themes such as survival and frontier life from a decidedly Eurocentric point of view, Prime Minister Trudeau's multiculturalism policy and its subsequent implementation led to a change in thematic focus. The Canadian Multiculturalism Act itself is not without problems, and has subsequently come under fire — as Neil Bissoondath demonstrates in *Selling Illusions*, it has the high aim of fostering cultural diversity alongside integration, of respecting cultural identity and equality, but is in itself a collection of generalizations that hide the true complexity of such an undertaking.[102] Likewise, Dieter Petzold points out, "We cannot force multiculturalism to mean that all ethnic elements present in a given country are strictly equal; to maintain a sense of identity, any nation must distinguish between dominant traits and marginal ones."[103] Nevertheless, the notion of multiculturalism has had a great impact on the production of children's literature, as both authors and critics have turned their attention to the depiction and representation of various ethnic and societal groups and cultural aspects.[104] A number of small publishing houses such as Tundra Books and Annick Press were founded in the 1970s with a focus on the production of multicultural national children's books — in other words, books that would reflect the new idea of a mosaic society while still promoting a distinctly Canadian identity.[105] Governmental funding now supports this diversity, giving a voice to those not of Anglo- or Franco-European descent, and encouraging regional, non-urban storytelling. Likewise, the rise of aboriginal publishing houses in the 1990s, such as Theytus Books or Pemmican Publications, which have made it their priority to publish the work of First Nations writers and illustrators, finally al-

102 Neil Bissoondath, *Selling Illusions: The Cult of Multiculturalism in Canada* (Toronto: Penguin, 1994) 39-42.

103 Dieter Petzold, "Multiculturalism in Canadian Children's Books: The Embarrassment of History," *Voices of the Other: Children's Literature and the Postcolonial Context*, ed. Roderick McGillis (New York: Garland, 2000) 178.

104 Edwards and Saltman.

105 Edwards and Saltman.

lowed First Nations people to tell their own stories, when they had previously only been depicted as part of legends and retellings of folk tales.[106]

Petzold rightly points out that education is central to multiculturalism — promoting knowledge and understanding, cultural sensitivity, and (implicit) instructions to cope with difficult situations.[107] As such, ethnocultural picturebooks are socio-political tools, perhaps more explicitly than other works of children's literature are. They are carriers of culture and ideology in a double and triple sense. Whereas in other types of picturebooks, values and norms might be less explicit or less focal in both the text and illustrations, the ethnocultural picturebook very consciously attempts to paint an authentic picture of a certain region or culture. The stories these books tell tend to be either problem narratives, portraying, for instance, the immigrant experience, poverty, loss of identity, and racism, or they are stories incorporating specific aspects of a culture, such as its mythology, history, or special traditions. Sometimes, both these intentions merge into a single narrative, as well, such as in Michael Kusugak's picturebook *Baseball Bats for Christmas*, which portrays the author's own childhood in the Inuit village of Repulse Bay, and at the same time shows the slow advance of Western customs and their growing influence on the community. Yet some critics are suspicious of these didactic messages and intentions, if not outright dismissive of them. "Children do not 'catch' morals, good or bad, from books, and it would be a shame if parents began to pop books down their children's throats like pills,"[108] Michele Landsberg writes in response to the rise of problem books. Although it is true that negative influence on children's behavior has often been cited in an attempt to ban children's and young adult books such as *Where The Wild Things Are* and *In The Night Kitchen* by Maurice Sendak in the US,109 or Joanne K. Rowling's *Harry*

106 Edwards and Saltman.

107 Petzold 178.

108 Michele Landsberg, qtd. in Waterston 79.

109 "100 Most Frequently Challenged Books: 1990-2000," *ALA.org*, 28 March 2008, American Library Association, 11 Dec. 2009 <http://www.ala.org/ala/issuesadvocacy/banned/frequentlychallenged/challengedbydecade/1990_2000.cfm>.

Potter and R. L. Stine's *Goosebumps* and *Fear Street* series in Canada,[110] it is undeniable that books do have an emotional impact on children, just as they do on adults. For example, many children tend to pick fictional characters from a variety of media (literature, television, comics, or video games) as role models or heroes, and, especially at a younger age, often engage in imitative acts such as "superhero play," in which they emulate their favorite characters.[111] Children live through books in the same manner, and the older they become, the more they do not only respond to the aesthetic qualities of a book, but also become affected by ideas, something Louise Rosenblatt describes as "efferent reading."[112] By extension, children are also likely to take away messages from ethnocultural narratives. These books are not cure-alls or miracle drugs, yet they may accomplish several important things. For one, they give children from specific ethnic backgrounds or certain regions representation which popular media such as television often do not give them. Many television series, real or animated, are lacking in characters of non-WASP backgrounds and thinking. For example, the popular animated American TV series *Avatar: The Last Airbender*, one of the few cartoon series extensively featuring characters based on Asian, Native American and Pacific island cultures, is now to be made into a live-action motion picture — a live-action motion picture with an almost exclusively white leading cast,[113] thereby effectively removing the representation of cultures which are marginalized in Western society. For another, these children's books address issues with which a lot of children are confronted in their lives, whether they are personally affected or not — themes such as racism, bullying, estrangement, isolation, loss, and rootlessness play a role in a great many lives, and are difficult to cope with at

110 "Challenged Books and Magazines List," *Freedom to Read*, Feb. 2009, Freedom of Expression Committee, 11 Dec. 2009 <http://www.freedomtoread.ca/docs/challenged_books_and_magazines.pdf>.

111 Kristin J. Anderson, "Parents or Pop Culture? Children's Heroes and Role Models," *Childhood Education* (Spring 2002) Findarticles.com. 11 Dec. 2009. <http://findarticles.com/p/articles/mi_qa3614/is_200204/ai_n9044749/>.

112 Louise Rosenblatt, qtd in Waterston 78.

113 Dan Zak, "In Va., Casting About for Mongolian Actors," *WashingtonPost.com,* 2 March 2009, The Washington Post, 11 Dec. 2009 <http://www.washingtonpost.com/wp-dyn/content/article/2009/03/01/AR2009030102088.html>.

best, even for adults. Beyond all possible positive reinforcement of values, cultural heritage or regional pride, what such books definitely do is expose children to other people, other places, and other cultures. And this is one of the main reasons why reading is regarded as a positive pastime, an activity worth pursuing no matter one's age, since books are said to expand one's horizon and encourage the richness of the mind.

4. Analysis

Having touched upon the complexities of some aspects of contemporary Canadian children's literature, this section will now turn to the analysis of ten selected Canadian picturebooks containing regional and ethnocultural themes. These books are Sheryl McFarlane's *Waiting for the Whales*, Michael Kusugak's *Baseball Bats for Christmas*, Troon Harrison's *Courage to Fly*, Andrea Spalding's *Solomon's Tree*, Rachna Gilmore's *A Gift for Gita*, Madeleine Thien's *The Chinese Violin*, Ian Wallace's *Duncan's Way*, David Bouchard's *The Dragon New Year*, Joy Kogawa's *Naomi's Tree*, and Jeanette Armstrong's *Neekna and Chemai*. They have been chosen to showcase the wide range of topics, illustrative styles, and regions or ethnicities to be found in contemporary Canadian children's picturebooks; however, they present only a fraction of a much wider and diversified field. To cover all the aspects of this field and all the aspects of Canadian society would go far beyond the scope of this thesis; indeed, as both literature and culture of any kind are ever-growing, it would likely be a never-ending task. Thus, the focus will rest on the ten books listed above, by first discussing them individually in order to show the thematic richness and the interplay between text and illustrations. Subsequently, the books will be examined together for common themes and symbols which will reflect certain Canadian issues, attitudes and trends. Special attention will be paid to the figure of the child in these texts, both as a character and as a carrier of perceptions of childhood.[114] Moreover, it should be noted that the analysis will stray away from standard critical concepts due to the nature of the texts involved. These texts primarily rely on schematic representation, symbolism, and ambiguity; therefore, it is necessary to reformulate and make visible their implications, meaning that the following examination will adhere more to the content level with an aim to reconstruct coherence than what might be appropriate for an adult text, or even a text without visual material.

---

114 None of the children's books chosen for this analysis contain page numbers. Therefore, a page count has been introduced to facilitate the retrieval of information.

4.1. *Waiting for the Whales*

Sheryl McFarlane's award-winning picturebook tells the story of an old man living by himself in a cottage by the sea. His only company are the orca whales who periodically arrive at the coast to feed, only to depart again. Their coming fills the old man with joy, just as their departure makes his own loneliness clear to him.[115] This routine is disrupted when his daughter abruptly arrives with her baby, and moves in with him again. Although the old man is reluctant at first, holding the baby causes him to remember holding his own children,[116] and he begins to warm up to the idea. The book continues to detail life at the cottage, as the baby grows up into a young girl, learning all her grandfather has to teach her.

On the surface, *Waiting for the Whales* is a tale of an old man with a void in his heart, which is filled by the arrival of his grandchild, and the grandchild herself, who is allowed to live out an idyllic childhood at the isolated hut by the sea. Ron Lightburn's realistic illustrations accompanying the text are full of refracting light and warm, earthy colors, supporting the impression of warmth and security created by the text. As shown in Fig. 1 below, the use of natural light particularly evokes an atmosphere of serenity which remains strong throughout all illustrations depicting the old man's interactions with his granddaughter. More importantly, Fig. 1 foregrounds the characters' preoccupation with each other as both guardian figures are shown directing all their attention at the child, a focus which is maintained throughout the illustrations depicting the old man's interactions with his granddaughter. Interestingly, Fig. 1 also marks the first and last time the old man is drawn gazing down at the child, who is resting in his arms and thus forced to look up at his face. In subsequent illustrations, the old man is shown making a conscious effort to remain on the same level as his grandchild, either by lifting her close to his face as an infant, or by bending down or towards her as she grows older, in order to ensure that his lessons can be observed perfectly from the child's vantage point.

115 Sheryl McFarlane, *Waiting for the Whales* (Victoria: Orca, 1991) 4.

116 McFarlane 12.

Fig. 1. The Old Man Receives a Visit; Ron Lightburn, from Sheryl McFarlane, *Waiting for the Whales* 13.

Nature is a friendly element; it provides the old man with work to do as he tills his "enormous garden,"[117] collects mussels and seaweed at the beach,[118] and harvests salal herb in the forests to sell to florist shops in town.[119] The forests are the forests of his childhood[120] — he knows them, has grown up playing in them, they are an extension of his home and provide no unknown or threatening elements. And through the old man's guidance, the land also becomes a cradle for his granddaughter. The first thing he does is to bring her to the shore as a baby in order to show her the arriv-

117 McFarlane 6.

118 McFarlane 8.

119 McFarlane 10.

120 McFarlane 10.

al of the orcas,[121] a wonder she is yet too young to understand. As she grows older, he continues to teach her, guiding her through the woods, showing her how to plant the garden, so that she may feel as secure in the vast expanse of nature as he does.

The outside world is notably absent from the narrative. Although McFarlane briefly mentions the old man selling or giving away his crops in town, the city life never intrudes upon the quiet life at the cottage. There are no neighbors, no acquaintances, and although the little girl presumably goes to school, the reader is never introduced to this sphere or any friends she might make. In fact, the narrative strongly suggests that she keeps to herself, with only her close family members for company. However, she does not appear to need more than that — the little girl grows up in a safe space, surrounded by love and wisdom. Although her grandfather is not depicted as the most affectionate man — he usually acts less than enthusiastic when spending time with her[122] — she seems to know his feelings, sticking to him "like glue."[123] McFarlane does not describe the girl in great detail, merely saying that, "The fat baby girl grew into a serious little girl, a wild little girl, a stubborn little girl."[124] Instead of showing these characteristics as problematic, they are meant to depict the little girl as a normal child, unafraid and sometimes unrestrained without being destructive. The illustrations only partly support the written characterization, as they usually depict the little girl listening quietly to her grandfather as he instructs her how to water crops[125] and explains woodland plants to her,[126] and how she then calmly carries out what he teaches her when he becomes too old to work.[127] The girl's mother is notably absent from the narrative as well as the illustrations for a good portion of the book. She does not seem to be the central figure in her daughter's life, and only starts to become important when the

---

121 McFarlane 14.

122 McFarlane 16.

123 McFarlane 16.

124 McFarlane 16.

125 McFarlane 17.

126 McFarlane 19.

127 McFarlane 21.

old man begins to feel the fatigue of age. Then, it is the mother who works in the garden with her daughter, who collects wood and herbs while the old man sits on the porch. When he dies on the very day the orcas arrive, the little girl cries bitter tears, but is consoled by her mother: "Don't be sad, sweet girl. Your grandfather's spirit has gone to leap and swim with the whales."[128] Here, the pictures and the text become contrastive — although the girl is immediately comforted by her mother, the images move from warm earthiness to cool gray tones and shadows, color seemingly draining from the little girl's life at the loss. Devastated, she is shown standing next to her grandfather's hat.[129] The loss of the grandfather causes the mother to regain importance in her daughter's life, as they wait out the winter months together, hoping for the orcas to return. The return of the orcas is also the return of color and warmth to the pictures, as the little girl notices a new calf swimming with the whales.[130] The sun returns, and the little girl is filled with joy once again, running to tell her mother of her discovery.

The little girl's idyllic childhood full of warmth and security is only threatened by the loss of her grandfather. However, the young protagonist manages to recover from this experience with her mother's love and the comfort that her grandfather's spirit indeed rests with the whales he loved so much, that he has perhaps even been reborn in the existence of the whale calf the girl spots that day. Despite this, the story carries a certain undertone of melancholy, the warmth and security seem tenuous, facilitated by the fact that the cottage is far from civilization. Throughout the story, the family unit is alone — as mentioned above, the outside world is tangential, deliberately excluded and unimportant in this circle of three. It seems to have little to no influence on the family life. This becomes especially important when one examines the circumstances under which the young mother comes to the cottage: She has not come to visit, she has not announced herself. She arrives without warning, holding only her baby and a bit of luggage.[131] McFarlane does not make her a central figure, nor does she explain the young mother's motivations. However, McFarlane still succeeds at painting

---

128 McFarlane 24.

129 McFarlane 25.

130 McFarlane 30.

131 McFarlane 12.

a much darker picture of the family circumstances. It is doubtful that the young woman has merely ended her relationship with the baby's father; she arrives at the doorstep with her bags packed, hoping that her own father will shelter her and her child. She and the old man do not appear to be on speaking terms prior to her arrival, as there is never any mention of contact between them. The old man is depicted as lonely and forgotten, never receiving a phone call or a letter from anyone. For the young woman to turn to her estranged father so unexpectedly, arriving only with a few belongings, hints quite strongly that she may be fleeing from an abusive partner or husband.

McFarlane presents a child who is headstrong and tomboyish, who is allowed to grow up free of worry. She gives her grandfather purpose and company again, and takes his disgruntled attitude for what it is — an old man uncertain how to show affection. In return, she learns from him, and from her mother, to a lesser extent. However, she is also being safeguarded more than she realizes, never learning of the circumstances that drove a wedge between her mother and grandfather so long ago, or the circumstances under which her mother arrives at the cottage. The little girl is never depicted as missing anything in her life — she does not ask for her father, and seems to have little interest in things outside the isolationist sphere surrounding her grandfather's cottage. This attitude appears to be her own; neither the mother nor grandfather are ever shown actively discouraging or keeping the little girl from exploring the world around her, but it stands to reason that the mother has deliberately chosen this remote and isolated location to keep her daughter safe from harm.

4.2. *Baseball Bats for Christmas*

Michael Arvaarluk Kusugak's picture book takes the reader to the settlement of Repulse Bay at the Arctic Circle in the not so distant past of 1955. The third person narrative depicts life in the town as seen from the perspective of Arvaarluk, a seven-year-old boy (who is quite possibly the author himself), and Arvaarluk's fascination with Christmas. Through the child's eyes, the story explores the influence of European culture on the Arctic North in a light and humorous tone, and the culture clash that happens when the local supply pilot brings the town a Christmas gift they have never seen before — trees.

Despite the fact that *Baseball Bats for Christmas* is ostensibly a Christmas tale, it also allows for a closer look at the changes taking place in Inuit life and Inuit culture in the 1950s. The illustrations accompanying the story suit its tone — a combination of watercolor and pencil artwork, Vladyana Krykorka's pictures manage to infuse even the icy North with warmth and color, creating a peaceful and almost luminescent ambience befitting Northern lights and sunsets. Although an unfamiliar reader would expect the North to be a hostile environment, neither Kusugak's narrative nor Krykorka's illustrations suggest that this is so. As the first story illustration in the book, Fig. 2 sets the theme of depicting the children at play, suggesting their familiarity with their surroundings, which, although frozen and covered in snow, convey the impression of a playground rather than a frozen wilderness. Furthermore, Fig. 2 also marks the trend towards a noticeable absence of adults from the story; although they are mentioned in the text in passing, they are rarely present in the pictures. In the text, they serve as role models and heroic figures, such as Rocky Parsons, the pilot, whom all the children adore because he supplies the town with outside goods and medicine. They are rule-makers and educators, such as Arvaarluk's mother, who admonishes him for trying to break the survey plaque, or Father Didier, the mission priest, who fulfills the role of a schoolteacher and nurse for the children of Repulse Bay. They are figures of authority, but it is a gentle authority, one that does not, as evident in Fig. 2, intrude upon the children's play time in any significant form, and, in fact, trusts the children to behave themselves and stay safe on their own.

Fig. 2. The Inuit Children at Play; Vladyana Krykorka, from *Baseball Bats for Christmas* (c) 1990 by Michael Arvaarluk Kusugak (text); (c) 1990 Vladyana Krykorka (art), published by Annick Press, Ltd.

As one of the children, Arvaarluk is as inclined towards fun and mischief as his friends. Even though he is described as "very asthmatic,"[132] this condition does not mark him as an outsider in the community or among the other children; he has friends and plays games like everyone else, even though running about demands a considerable amount of strength.[133] Despite his condition, Arvaarluk is inquisitive, enthusiastic and sometimes mischievous. The Inuit experience of Western culture is described through his eyes, and the narrative adopts a humorous, slightly surreal tone whenever Arvaarluk is confronted with unfamiliar objects whose purpose he

132 Michael Arvaarluk Kusugak, *Baseball Bats for Christmas* (Vancouver: Annick, 1990) 4.

133 Kusugak 4, 20.

cannot guess, such as the geographical survey plate that has recently been installed to mark the Arctic circle just outside Repulse Bay, and which the children playfully try to dislodge. When his mother tries to forbid the game by saying, "If you knock that brass plate off that rock, the whole world will come to a terrible end,"[134] Arvaarluk is not deterred in the least. He imagines the Earth bouncing wildly through space like a seal float losing air, and tries all the harder to make it fall off.[135] This example serves to illustrate a prominent narrative feature; the text is meant to replicate the mindset and voice of a seven-year-old child, mimicking the sounds of the supply plane landing and subsequent refueling with onomatopoeia,[136] turning nouns into verbs (e.g. "Peter 'Happy Nuuyaed' him a pair of caribou-skin mitts"[137]) and causally connecting events in the wrong order. For instance, Arvaarluk thinks that the raising of the Union Jack will lead the supply plane to return rather than the other way around, and believes that the singing of Christmas songs in church is what causes Christmas to arrive.[138]

The world Arvaarluk grows up in presents an intriguing mix of Western influences and traditional Inuit ways. Although the people are still largely depicted wearing fur clothing and moccasins, there are instances when the illustrations show them wearing Western clothing such as plaid shirts and jeans with suspenders.[139] The people travel around on dog sleds, yet rely on Rocky Parsons, the pilot, to restock supplies in town.[140] In winter, they live in sod huts and igloos, the mission being the only building in town with electric lights and heating, pictures of the Pope and Queen Elizabeth hanging from the walls.[141] Although hardly anyone speaks English, they still sing English Christmas songs like, "O come all ye faithful,"[142] and have

134 Kusugak 6.

135 Kusugak 6.

136 Kusugak 8-9.

137 Kusugak 14.

138 Kusugak 9, 12.

139 Kusugak 12.

140 Kusugak 8-9.

141 Kusugak 12.

142 Kusugak 12.

adapted Christmas to suit their own customs better. "Christmas was a time when you took your most favourite thing in the world and gave it to your very best friend,"[143] Arvaarluk explains. The gifts are often tools and other useful things — caribou-skin mitts, a telescope — prompting the narrator to tell of his father's misfortune during the gift exchange, when he receives an untamed dog in return for his only telescope. The dog promptly escapes and stays away for an entire year, until Arvaarluk's father finally manages to lure it in and catch it with a lasso, training it to become "the best lead dog they ever had."[144] Arvaarluk and his friends incorporate elements from both worlds into their daily lives, playing with traditional toys just as they do with toy guns and rubber balls, enthusiastic about Christian festivals and the arrival of the supply plane, dreaming of one day being allowed to fly in the sky together with Rocky Parsons.[145] The Western world leaving traces in their lives is not perceived or depicted as a threat, but rather a new way to invent games. Until Rocky Parsons brings them to Repulse Bay in 1955, the children have never seen a Christmas tree, or any tree at all. They eventually identify the needle-bearing green objects as "standing-ups"[146] which they know from picturebooks, but are still not quite certain what to make of them. Eventually, the children decide to completely divert the trees from their intended use by carving bats from their trunks and branches, since there is hardly ever enough wood to make proper baseball bats.[147] They spend the year having fun batting balls around, "making more bats with the spindly trees when they broke."[148] One can only assume that the mission priest did not have the heart to inform them of the true purpose of Christmas trees, as the book ends with Arvaarluk and his friends enthusiastically looking forward to receiving "baseball bats for Christmas"[149] once again.

143 Kusugak 14.

144 Kusugak 16.

145 Kusugak 8.

146 Kusugak 10.

147 Kusugak 18.

148 Kusugak 23.

149 Kusugak 23.

4.3. *Courage to Fly*

Troon Harrison's picture book deals with the life of Meg, a small girl from the Caribbean islands, who has recently arrived in Canada with her family. The book follows Meg as she fights a losing battle against the fear of the new country, hiding away in the safety of her own room. Only when she comes across an injured swallow does she slowly become more confident in herself and dares to venture outside once more.

Courage to Fly depicts the experience of an immigrant child in a country that is foreign and frightening to her. Zhong-Yang Huang's sprawling watercolor illustrations that accompany the story often take up the majority of a double page, conveying a sense of space and scale similar to what a small girl might feel, lost in a large, foreign metropolis. Although the city itself is not painted in a particularly threatening manner, with patches of greenery, sunlight glinting off the skyscrapers and city birds fluttering every which way (see Fig. 3), Meg is shown fleeing from the overwhelming presence of the buildings, or carefully inching along their corners. Contributing to the sense of isolation is the fact that Meg is usually depicted alone, avoiding the company of other children (Fig. 3) and maintaining her distance from the adults in the story. In most illustrations, the only thing smaller and more easily startled than her are the birds, who, like Meg, blindly flutter off when disturbed. The reader never learns what exactly sparks Meg's extreme anxiety, as the narrative does not mention a specific incident or negative impression that might have caused the little girl to withdraw from the world. Meg merely appears to be overwhelmed by everything — the size of the city, the people, the sounds: "Apartment towers were dark fingers blocking the sun. Long shadows lay across the afternoon street when Meg came home from school. Her feet hurried past roaring gratings. Sirens wailed. Strangers jostled her."[150] The images also place Meg in opposition to other children in her neighborhood, who seem perfectly at ease in the midst of this auditory and visual pandemonium, riding their bikes, playing tag or otherwise capering around outdoors (Fig. 3).

---

150 Troon Harrison, *Courage to Fly*, 1st paperback edition, (Calgary: Red Deer, 2006) 2.

Fig. 3. Meg Running Towards Safety; Zhong-Yang Huang,
from Troon Harrison, *Courage to Fly* 2.

Her only shelter appears to be within her room in the family apartment, watching the streets from a safe distance, and although she goes to school, she hates having to go outside, always running home as quickly as she can.[151] Although there is proof that the new city is not nearly as frightening as she thinks it is, Meg's fear has adopted a dynamic of its own, rendering her unable to face the world. Jenny, a neighbor's child, often comes to invite her to play with her, yet Meg continues to reject the offer, incapable of even considering braving the outside, until Jenny stops trying to befriend her.[152] Her uncontrollable and very obvious fear sadly also makes Meg an

151 Harrison 4.

152 Harrison 5.

easy target for bullies at school, who begin to follow her home, throwing things after her and calling her names.[153]

From the start, Harrison weaves the metaphor of the bird into Meg's characterization with the aim of illustrating the child's mindset. Meg "huddles small inside herself like a frightened bird,"[154] "scuttles" and "shrinks,"[155] and the reader can easily imagine her voice as thin as a peep when she speaks, barely above a whisper. Meg envies the birds their freedom, watching them fly from her bedroom window, just as she envies the children, who "swoop by" in the street below.[156] When she meets an old man performing tai-chi in the park, that metaphor is extended even further, as the old man seems to know exactly what is going on in Meg's heart, and is using his exercises to mirror her feelings: "'This is a move called Lonely Goose Leaves Flock,' he said, and Meg nodded. She knew how that goose felt. 'And this move is called Wild Horse Chases Wind,' he told her. Meg remembered how her legs used to gallop through happier days."[157] Her meeting with a real bird seems almost inevitable at this point. When Meg finds a swallow half-frozen in the snow, she takes it home to care for it, diligently feeding and warming it, even arranging a comfortable little box for it to sleep in.[158] The bird almost becomes an extension of herself — Meg longs to guard it from the outside world, keeping it with her all the time and refusing to let it go.[159] However, when the weather clears up, doubts begin to befall her despite her vehement protests of keeping the bird confined to her room. She takes the swallow to the old man, asking him whether the bird can survive inside the box.[160] The question is almost rhetorical — Meg seems to feel that her desire to keep the bird caged is wrong,

---

153 Harrison 7.

154 Harrison 2.

155 Harrison 7.

156 Harrison 4.

157 Harrison 8.

158 Harrison 14.

159 Harrison 17.

160 Harrison 19.

but still longs for the old man to tell her that it is the right choice. Once again, the old man uses tai-chi to explain why the swallow needs freedom:

> "This move is called Swallow Skims Water… and this one is Swallow Penetrates the Clouds. There are no clouds and no lakes inside a box." "But outside — maybe it will die," said Meg. "Ah, maybe," the old man agreed. "But in a box, it will die for certain. You have to give the swallow its chance. It has the courage it needs to fly."[161]

Eventually, Meg realizes that caging the swallow forever would be a cruel choice, and begs Jenny and the old man to come with her when she frees the bird. As the swallow happily lifts off into the sunshine, Meg once again feels a connection to the bird — its joy is infectious and seeing it fly fills her with happiness.[162] This gives Meg courage; she finds she is able to smile at Jenny, and when Jenny decides to extend another offer of friendship to her, she finally decides that it is much better to accept. The story ends with the two girls playing on the swings, swinging higher and higher, a metaphor for Meg's own flight to freedom.[163]

What is particularly interesting about the story is that the adults that should be close to Meg are almost entirely absent from the narrative. Meg's father never makes an appearance, and her mother only briefly does when she brings home the swallow, helping her to care for it. The illustrations and text depict her as a kindly woman whose time is consumed by housework and caring for her infant son.[164] It is not quite clear why she does nothing to encourage her daughter to go outside — perhaps she has tried in the past and has given up, perhaps she is too preoccupied to notice, perhaps she is not sure how to approach her own child. In contrast, the old Chinese man seems almost like a magician, able to guess Meg's worry after seeing her for only a short time, and using a peculiar way — tai-chi moves — to make her own dilemma clear to her. His calm, grandfatherly wisdom draws Meg in and allows her to see the old man as a confidant, but he does not interfere with her decisions. The cryptic stories he tells her require Meg to think

---

161 Harrison 21.

162 Harrison 27.

163 Harrison 28.

164 Harrison 12-13.

on her own and decide what she deems best, and it is exactly through this non-interference that Meg finally learns to be courageous. The old man remains mysterious until the end — his name and motivations are never revealed, and the last scene shows him watching the playing girls, his final advice more intended for the reader than Meg: "'This move is called Wild Geese Flying In Pairs,' he murmured, his arms as light and flexible as wings."[165]

4.4. *Solomon's Tree*

Andrea Spalding's picturebook tells the story of Solomon, a young Tsimshian boy, and the maple tree he loves so much. When the old tree is felled by a storm and subsequently used as firewood, Solomon is heartbroken. But his uncle has a unique way of cheering him up — he will revive the spirit of the tree by carving a ritual mask from one of its logs. *Solomon's Tree* is a story about a child's spiritual bond with nature, carried from a very concrete level to a more abstract level. The full-page illustrations by Janet Wilson are realistic oil paintings, the text on the accompanying page often decorated with smaller pictures and frames including Tsimshian artwork. In the epilogue, Spalding states that the decorations were provided by Tsimshian master carver Victor Reece, who designed an elongated raven for these panels since "Raven is the trickster and storyteller for Tsimshian tradition."[166] The strong colors and shading techniques render tangible both the vibrant life of the maple tree and the physicality of the woodcraft in later parts of the story (see Fig. 4), while the use of earthy hues throughout the images underscores the idea of transformation, the transfer or reincarnation of the maple's essence in the wooden mask. Solomon and his family are depicted as uniting Western elements with elements of their own culture (see Fig. 4); their clothing, although largely Westernized, shows elements of their heritage at times — for example, Solomon is shown wearing a t-shirt with a printing of Tsimshian ritual drawing on it,[167]

---

165 Harrison 31.

166 Spalding 31.

167 Spalding 23.

and his grandmother is seen wearing a jacket with traditional patterns[168] — and Solomon's uncle is said to use both traditional carving tools and chainsaws for his woodwork.[169]

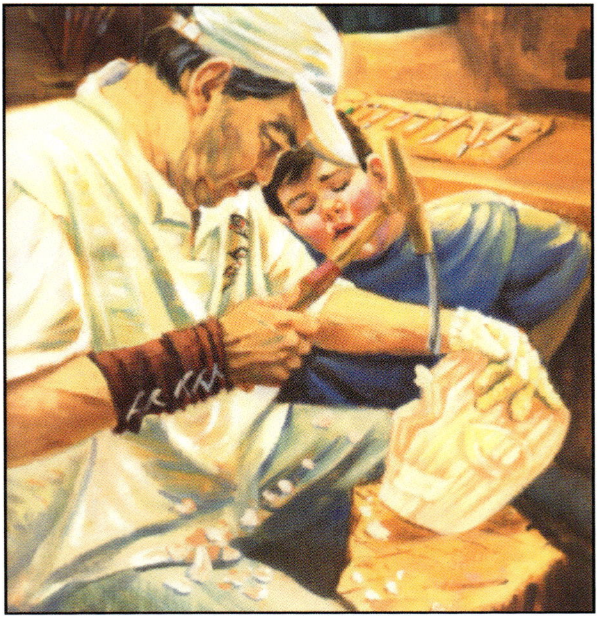

Fig. 4. Solomon Watching His Uncle Carve the Mask; Janet Wilson, from Andrea Spalding, *Solomon's Tree* 21.

Solomon's bond with his favorite maple tree is reminiscent of the way some children behave towards plants and animals, considering them friends and holding conversations with them. Coupled with the illustrations, Spalding manages to craft a very thoughtful and heart-warming picture of this friendship by showing the two-way communication between the boy and the tree. Just as Solomon speaks to the tree with words, the tree answers with its own language — rustling, creaking, swaying in the wind — which Solo-

168 Spalding 19.

169 Spalding 20.

mon interprets as replies to his words. He loves to climb the tree and hug it, its branches seemingly moving to embrace him in return.[170] The tree is treated as a person, fully capable of doing things one would traditionally ascribe to humans, such as playing, guiding or comforting. The maple conceals many secrets among its twigs and in its bark, small treasures of nature invisible to the casual observer, and guides Solomon to where they are hidden. The little boy is delighted and amazed by these discoveries — a hummingbird's nest with its small eggs, butterflies hatching from their chrysalis in the tree's bark. Instead of revealing these wonders to others, Solomon becomes the maple's confidant, vowing to keep his knowledge to himself: "'You mustn't tell,' whispered the tree. 'I promise,' Solomon whispered back."[171] Apart from these quiet observations, the tree also provides Solomon with wilder and more enthusiastic entertainment come autumn: "In fall the maple shed its golden leaves and winged seeds and rustled and chuckled as it showered Solomon. Solomon chased the dancing propellers and gathered together piles of leaves."[172] Even in winter, the tree isn't silent, "creak[ing] out lullabies" to lull the boy to sleep.[173]

Eventually, however, the old maple falls prey to a vicious storm. Solomon, terrified by the howling wind, hears how the tree meets its end: "CRAAACK. The maple gave a last despairing cry, crashed over the woodshed, and fell silent."[174] Although Solomon is heart-broken over the loss of his friend, he nonetheless has to help with the clean-up as his family cuts up the fallen tree to use as firewood and burn the scattered branches. In contrast to many other stories incorporating the element of a non-human, inanimate or even invisible friend, Solomon's family does not ridicule his behavior or consider it abnormal and worrisome. Once the work is done, his father gives him the last remaining maple log and takes him to his uncle, who has his own

170 Spalding 6.

171 Spalding 8-9.

172 Spalding 11.

173 Spalding 11.

174 Spalding 15.

ideas about consoling the child: he offers Solomon to show him the spirit of his beloved tree through the carving of a wooden mask.[175]

At this point, the focus shifts from Solomon's relationship with the maple tree to his relationship with his uncle. Although the maple remains important to Solomon, it is now his uncle who becomes his guide and instructs him how to craft a mask. The illustrations show the boy watching closely and learning how to use the tools, making it not quite clear how much he knows about his uncle's craft. For example, although he is inexperienced with the tools, he seems to be familiar with the ritual dance his uncle performs before starting his work. When the drum sounds and his uncle asks the ancestors for guidance, Solomon joins in with his own prayer:

> Gwā eee dim haoou,
> Here is what I have to say:
> Tree, let your spirit guide Uncle's fingers,
> Let those fingers show your face,
> Let your face help my memory,
> Let my memory always honor you.[176]

The uncle asks very specific questions about the tree, such as its scent, the animals hiding in its branches, and its voice, in order to craft the mask more accurately. Here, Solomon feels comfortable sharing the secrets he promised not to tell, as they will help to shape the mask.[177] Step by step, the mask begins to take shape, Solomon barely able to reign in his impatience but determined to do things exactly as told. When the mask has finally been dried, painted, and oiled, the spirit of the tree has been given shape: "The wood sprang to life and smiled up at him. 'Hello, tree,' whispered Solomon. 'Hello, Solomon,' the mask whispered back."[178] The story ends with Solomon putting on his mask and dancing to the beat of his uncle's drum, awakening a dormant maple seed deep in the earth.[179]

175 Spalding 16.

176 Spalding 17.

177 Spalding 21.

178 Spalding 27.

179 Spalding 30.

4.5. *A Gift for Gita*

Rachna Gilmore's picturebook tells the story of Gita, a young girl from India, whose family has moved to Canada. Despite their starting problems, they eventually settle down, and Gita is able to come to terms with her new home. When her grandmother arrives for a visit from India, however, the family is faced with a difficult choice: to remain in the new country, or return to their beloved homeland.

A Gift for Gita is a very quiet and non-dramatic tale of a child coming to terms with her dual identity as an immigrant. Gita is old enough to have many memories of India, and has been in Canada for a sufficiently long time to have made memories there, causing her to struggle with her mixed feelings about leaving and staying. Alice Priestley's illustrations are colored pencil sketches employing the hachure technique, permitting a great contrast between foreground and background, as seen in Fig. 5. Here, the characters are rendered strongly in the foreground, with clear lines to frame their figures and any objects nearby. The background, however, remains hazy, at times almost lending the images the impression of a picture stage (see Fig. 5). Usually, the images are close-ups of the characters in the story; only twice does Priestley opt for a more removed outside perspective slightly reminiscent of film technique, such as when she chooses to draw the family as silhouettes seen through the living room window.[180] The warm, yellow-reddish tone of the images causes Gita to stand out in her blue jeans and sweater. Another prominent theme are autumn-reddened maple leaves — almost every picture in the book features them in some manner or another, as shady blurs peeking in through the windows (see Fig. 5) or twining in the foreground as Gita sits outside. In fact, only two out of twelve images do not feature them at all, namely when Gita is alone with her grandmother, which serves as an interesting, silent separator of the spaces "Canada" and "India."

---

180 Rachna Gilmore, *A Gift for Gita* (Toronto: Second Story, 1998) 7.

Fig. 5. Gita Embracing Her Grandmother; Alice Priestley,
from Rachna Gilmore, *A Gift for Gita* 5.

The reader is first introduced to Gita when she is sitting in the living room, playing with the sari-clad nesting dolls her grandmother — whom she calls "Naniji" — has brought along as a gift. She is brimming with happiness over her grandmother's visit, determined to spend as much time with her as possible.[181] However, the jovial atmosphere abruptly sobers when her father reveals that he has received a letter offering him the job as head of a new branch back in India. At first, Gita is overjoyed at the thought of seeing her homeland again and returning to live with her grandmother, but then the realization dawns that she will have to leave her friends in Canada behind.[182] In the ensuing silence, she anxiously observes her family's reactions — her grandmother's hopeful apprehension, her mother's shock, her father's evasiveness. The last straw is when she sees her grandmother's fake

181 Gilmore 4.

182 Gilmore 8.

smile, "the way she had smiled when they were leaving India."[183] Unable to cope with the tension anymore, she runs outside to hide under her favorite maple tree. Worriedly, she begins to contemplate her dilemma, "When had she stopped missing India? When she and Amy became friends? When she first skated on the frozen canal?"[184] The nesting doll becomes a metaphor for the layers of recollections and fragments of her identity, and as she dissembles it, Gita realizes that the memories of Canada feel more immediate, clearer than her connection to India. That causes her to become all the more anxious, guilt over betraying her grandmother blending with fear of being taken to India against her will. She runs back to her family, desperately begging her parents to stay. It turns out that her fear is unfounded, as her parents have indeed decided to remain. They have "put down roots,"[185] as her father phrases it, but this does not ease Gita's guilt over her grandmother: "'Naniji, I want to be with you, but…' she held the doll against her heart. 'Everything's here. Everything, but you'."[186] She tries to convince Naniji to stay, but even that decision has been made without her. Her parents have already tried to invite her grandmother, but she has refused, and gently explains her choice to Gita: "'My home's back in India,' she said softly. 'I love it there, just as you love it here. It's where I belong. All the parts of my life are there, and all my memories — everything except you'."[187] Gita tries to insist that she could make new memories here, but her grandmother cannot be swayed; she has made her new memories, which she will take back to India. At this point, her grandmother embraces her, promising that a part of her will always be with Gita, just like a part of Gita will always be with her.[188] Slowly, Gita comes to realize that she cannot have everything her heart desires, because others have to do what they desire, as well. She hands her grandmother the small, central nesting doll to take back, resolving to believe her words.[189]

---

183 Gilmore 10.

184 Gilmore 12.

185 Gilmore 10.

186 Gilmore 18.

187 Gilmore 20.

188 Gilmore 22.

189 Gilmore 24.

Although Gita is surrounded by an understanding and loving family, the story also makes clear a child's lack of influence over such a complex situation. Gita is preoccupied with her own worries, just as the adults are preoccupied with theirs, unable to comfort their child as they struggle to make a decision. And it is a decision they reach on their own, despite what Gita's father originally promises. Even though it turns out to be what Gita is secretly hoping for, her parents, at this point, do not know that. One could argue that they have observed their daughter and feel that they know what she would want, but this is hardly a certainty. In this sense, the story reflects the workings of many real-world families. Although children are allowed to voice their wishes, the final verdict is still delivered by the parents, as they ultimately have to decide on technicalities such as work, money, education and the possibilities for their children's future, even if it happens to oppose their children's momentary desires. In Gita's case, each decision demands a sacrifice from the family in general and Gita in particular, as it means deciding between her friends and the country she has come to love on the one hand, and her grandmother and former home on the other hand. Thus, it is perhaps better that Gita is allowed to discover her feelings on the matter on her own, without being swept up in a discussion that might include concepts and aspects beyond her control, where the adults are forced to pay attention to the matter at hand rather than to their worried child.

4.6. *The Chinese Violin*

Madeleine Thien's book tells the story of Lin Lin, a small Chinese girl who moves to Canada together with her father. The story traces their fate from leaving behind their life in China, through the hardships they have to endure in the foreign country to the eventual sliver of hope, as the small family slowly begins to overcome their problems, allowing them to feel more at home in Canada.

The Chinese Violin deals with the darker side of emigrating to a new country — the language barrier, loneliness, racism and poverty, and does so very implicitly at times. Joe Chang's wax crayon illustrations have a very iconic feel to them — the characters are drawn with barely any defining features, their expressions sometimes exaggerated to compensate for this, giving the impression that they could be anyone rather than specific people with a very specific fate (see Fig. 6). The colors stand in stark contrast to the brown background, with splashes of white, black, green and red to offset the uniform background. This lends the illustrations a certain austere feel which is sometimes in opposition to the text, particularly during descriptions of the verdant landscape. In fact, this trend is only broken in the illustration accompanying Lin Lin's school concert (shown in Fig. 6), which features a very strongly colored background to emphasize Lin Lin's stage presence, who is now clad in a bright yellow and fairly elaborate dress, which marks her own personal transformation.

Fig. 6. Lin Lin Playing the Violin in Concert; Joe Chang, from Madeleine Thien, *The Chinese Violin* 28.

The story opens with descriptions of Lin Lin's daily life in rural China. The village is shown to be an idyllic place filled with "butterflies and birds and flowers,"[190] where people enjoy gathering and playing their musical instruments. Lin Lin loves listening to her father play the violin, its tunes mingling with the noises from the village and often lulling the little girl to sleep.[191] However, the narrative soon shows that Lin Lin's happy impressions are offset by her father's decision to emigrate to Canada. It is not clear why he chooses to do so — it might be due to poverty or the wish to allow his daughter to have better educational and financial possibilities — but the text focuses on Lin Lin's confusion and fear instead of her father's reasons. Lin Lin puts on a façade of excitement, but is terrified to leave her home behind.[192] She seems to know that she won't be seeing it again soon, or perhaps not ever, and walks through the village in hopes of being able to memorize the sights, and, more importantly, the sounds. The keening melody of a violin drifts towards her almost like a goodbye.[193]

This emphasis on sound-images persists as Lin Lin and her father arrive in Vancouver to start their new life. Lin Lin is baffled and overwhelmed by the new sounds — new animals, new items, a new language. At school, she feels like an outsider, as the children are all speaking English to each other, playing foreign games, and even their laughter seems exclusive to Lin Lin, who stands lonely by herself. Here is also the first occasion that the illustration does not quite seem to match the text — in the picture, their arrival feels peaceful. The characters are smiling gently as they stroll down the sidewalk of a suburb in Vancouver, not appearing to be as bewildered and out of their depth as the text suggests.[194] This is mitigated by the neighboring page, which describes Lin Lin's experiences at school, the picture dominated entirely by her sad, worried face.[195] To take their mind away from the difficulties, her father brings them to a seaside park, claiming, "'Everyone says the park will make us feel at home again'."[196] When he be-

---

190 Madeleine Thien, *The Chinese Violin* (Vancouver: Whitecap, 2002) 2.

191 Thien 5.

192 Thien 6.

193 Thien 7.

194 Thien 8.

195 Thien 9.

196 Thien 10.

gins playing a song on the violin he has brought with him, Lin Lin feels her spirits starting to lift. When she falls asleep to the music, she has a highly symbolic dream — she is flying through the sky, able to see both her home village and Vancouver, separated by the ocean, but neither of them invisible. For the first time, she feels a sense of hope, and draws on the memory to comfort her as she continues to struggle at school.[197] However, things soon take a turn for the worse. Although the narrative does not say so directly, Lin Lin's father is unemployed, unable to support himself and his daughter, and thus takes them to a street corner to earn some money as a street performer. As the story is told from Lin Lin's perspective, she does not really seem to understand their situation and poverty — to her, everything in the country is strange, so giving a street performance with her father is by far not the strangest thing — in fact, she finds his presence comforting, the sound of his feet on the sidewalk "reassuring."[198] Here is the second time that the illustration does not match the text. The picture shows Lin Lin's father from behind, looking out at the street. The road is empty save for cars, and the single pedestrian is turning her back to his music, walking away without a glance. The narrative, however, describes people standing in a circle, admiring his talent and giving him change. This discrepancy might suggest that it has taken a long time to gather an audience.

As father and daughter are walking home, they are attacked by thugs who take away their earnings and destroy the Chinese violin. The father weeps brokenly, deprived of his last means to provide for his daughter. Lin Lin is unable to comfort him and unable to concentrate on her schoolwork, escaping into the past when she used to play in her village.[199] The story then abruptly leaps forward to show that Lin Lin's father has managed to find a new job as dishwasher — although he is very busy, he helps his daughter with her homework, promising her that this place will "feel like home" very soon.[200] From this point on, things seem to become easier. Lin Lin is determined to help her father by doing her best to improve at school, and eventually, her father manages to earn enough to buy his daughter a new

---

197 Thien 12.

198 Thien 14.

199 Thien 18.

200 Thien 20.

violin. Lin Lin is overjoyed at the gift and begins to practice everywhere. Through her playing, she begins to make friends, and eventually gets elected to perform in the school auditorium. When she sees all the familiar people in the audience, cheering and clapping, her own spirits lift, and she can feel her heart "singing."[201]

4.7. *Duncan's Way*

This picturebook by Ian Wallace tells the story of the young boy Duncan and his family, who are living along the Newfoundland coast in the aftermath of the collapse of the local fishing industry. With his father unemployed and depressed, the family is slowly forced to accept the thought of moving away to find a new life elsewhere, until Duncan thinks of an idea that might restore happiness to his father and allow them to stay.

Duncan's Way showcases the dwindling prosperity and slow depopulation of the Newfoundland coastal regions through the fate of a single family. Wallace's realistic colored pencil illustrations often make a point of showing the region's features, such as the grass- and rock-covered hills sloping towards the shore, the relatively Spartan-looking houses, and the prominent fishing docks. The muted colors draw the reader's eye, conveying a feeling of quietness bordering on transience which befits the tone of the story. The world in which Duncan is growing up is slowly crumbling, fading away. The small village is becoming steadily emptier as the people leave to find employment elsewhere, and those that are not leaving have to change their ways to adapt. Great changes have also happened to Duncan's family — for seven generations, the men of have worked as fishermen, and his father is the first who has been forced to abandon the tradition, overfishing destroying the stock of codfish most of the rural communities need to survive. "The cod had disappeared from the ocean's depths, and with them went a way of life,"[202] Wallace writes with finality, painting a scene of desolation, the single seagull circling overhead comparable to the few people who still remain. Despite this, eleven-year-old Duncan is portrayed as lively and energetic: although the situation is bad, he has not given up yet, unlike his

201 Thien 31.

202 Ian Wallace, *Duncan's Way* (Toronto: Groundwood, 2000) 4.

father, who seems to have completely lost his drive. Listlessly, he evades his son's attempts to engage him in any activity at all, until Duncan storms off, frustrated and at the end of his wits.[203]

Surprisingly, he withdraws to the town graveyard, a rather morbid choice of a hiding place. He is not afraid, however; the graveyard is a source of comfort to him and allows him to think of his options, surrounded by the tombstones of his long-deceased relatives. Given the setting that Wallace has chosen, the image seems like the physical equivalent to the metaphorically dying town. It is here that Duncan eventually arrives at the conclusion that the only way to draw his father out of his depression is to get him back on a boat, with the Atlantic as the only witness to his heartfelt promise.[204] With this resolve in mind, he returns home. His house is dominated by his father's apathy, who has completely withdrawn into his own world, envying the people winning money in game shows, and paying no attention to Duncan and his older brother. Although the children play and scuffle, they are always aware of their father's condition.[205] Even Duncan's mother has begun to share her husband's despair. A hard-working and loving woman, she is plagued by worry for the future, yet becomes extremely defensive when Duncan tells her of his idea.

> "But he does nothing except watch TV or stand at the side of the road talking to his buddies." His mother's body tensed. Duncan's eyes scanned the six loaves of bread on the counter. The four partridgeberry pies. And the plate of tea buns. "And bake." "Baking is hard work, too!" she snapped, and turned off the stove. "Supper's ready."[206]

She appears resigned to the inevitable, and discussing her husband's unhealthy behavior is almost too much for her. After dinner, she takes both her sons out to the beach, where "the largest iceberg they could remember"[207] has floated into the bay, sitting there unmoving and for all to see, symbolic of the insurmountable problem the family is facing. There, she

203 Wallace 4.

204 Wallace 8.

205 Wallace 10.

206 Wallace 12.

207 Wallace 12.

informs them of the plans to leave Newfoundland and move to the city in the vague hope of eking out a living elsewhere. Both children have been dreading this moment, and desperately beg their mother to stay. Duncan cannot imagine giving up his beloved hometown and the sea for a foreign place, no matter where it is in Canada. "We can't leave. We've been here forever,"[208] he finally chokes out, but his protest is defeated by the fact that the family cannot survive on the mother's income alone.

Duncan's Way puts a not so ordinary boy in an extraordinary situation. Duncan is portrayed as stubborn, determined and imaginative, characteristics that become important assets in the difficult time he goes through. His father's depression affects him deeply, to the point where he can barely think about anything else. Despite the fact that his older brother and mother are similarly affected, Duncan is the only one who tries to talk about the situation in a straightforward manner, who, indeed, sees no sense in not talking about it, while his mother is ensnared by the painful immediacy of the situation and reacts harshly when the very thing she knows to be there is made real by speaking about it. It is also noteworthy that although Luke, Duncan's brother, is portrayed as being several years older than him (presumably in his mid-teens) he appears to be just as helpless as the rest of the family. Despite the fact that the two brothers are on good terms, Duncan does not share his thoughts and worries with him, instead preferring to try and solve the problem on his own. One can assume at this point that perhaps he has tried to do so in the past and has been similarly rebuffed, or that Duncan's single-minded determination simply leads him to seek his answers on his own, without help. And it appears to be this determination that allows him to understand so clearly what his father needs, and to try out unconventional ideas to solve the dilemma. His parents and brother are too close to the problem — they face the reality of financial hardship, problems of work or education, which are most likely less immediate and more abstract for Duncan. Although he fears losing his home, as well, he is still able to approach the difficulties head-on, while the rest of his family is trapped inside the proverbial box, unable to think outside of it.

---

208 Wallace 14.

After a night of nightmares in which he imagines the entire stretch of coast dead, the lifeless fishing boats sitting abandoned on the shore, Duncan decides to try harder than ever. Alone, he drives a boat across the bay to visit Mr. Marshall, a retired fisherman whom he befriended long ago. When asked for advice, Mr. Marshall tosses Duncan a toy boat and asks him a question in return, "What is a boat, if not for fishing?"[209] As Duncan ponders the question, he realizes that a boat does not necessarily have to be used in just one way — it can serve as a means of transportation, a courier vessel. However, when it comes to the question of what Duncan's father could transport to people with his boat, Duncan is stumped once again. Momentarily, it is him who can only see the immediate situation, his father's silence and listlessness the most prominent thing he can think of, until it dawns on him that his father still likes to bake. "'If a garage can be a video store,' Duncan began slowly, 'can a boat be…' He set the tiny fishing boat back in the ocean. 'A bakery?'"[210] With this new plan in mind, Duncan sets out home. The rough sea is beginning to calm, and Duncan swerves around the large iceberg with ease, which coincides with the easing of his inner turmoil. Now that he has found a way, the future no longer looks quite so frightening, and the iceberg is no longer an overwhelming obstacle.

When he reveals his new idea to his family, they are surprisingly agreeable to such a risky plan. Even his father, after a moment of tense silence, agrees to give it a try, some measure of good humor entering his expression again as he begins to warm up to the thought of being a seafaring baker. Turning their fishing boat into a floating bakery consumes their last savings, which would leave them in quite a difficult position should Duncan's plan fail, yet everyone decides to work together with newfound hope. They outfit the boat with all the necessary equipment and even decide to rename it to "Duncan's Way"[211] to show their gratitude and acknowledgement. The book ends on a fairly ambiguous note — the closing scene shows the family setting out on the bakery boat for the very first time, the mother at the wheel, the father and sons baking bread and pies, all cheerful as they used to be and full of hope. Whether their new enterprise succeeds financially or

209 Wallace 20.

210 Wallace 22.

211 Wallace 28.

not is left entirely to the imagination of the reader, as the important point is that it has succeeded on a different and much more valuable scale: it has managed to pull the father out of his lethargy and restore his smile, the true goal of Duncan's plan.

4.8. *The Dragon New Year: A Chinese Legend*

The Dragon New Year, written by David Bouchard, spins a story from old Chinese legends to explain how the Chinese New Year celebration came to be. On the evening of Lunar New Year, a grandmother tells a frightened little girl the legend of the mythical dragon "New Year" and his defeat at the hands of Buddha in order to soothe the child to sleep. Bouchard's book combines the narrative framework and the embedded story with Zhong-Yang Huang's realistic oil paintings to craft an atmosphere reminiscent of fairytales, frequently dominating an entire double-page. Although text and image are generally kept side by side, they merge during specific scenes to convey a particularly immersive sense of movement and totality. The different brush stroke techniques create fluid, lively images which are often so vibrant that the reader's eye is inevitably drawn to them first instead of the text. In fact, given the size of the paintings, one could very well say that the text is merely supplementary, supporting the images rather than the other way around.

One detail which bears mentioning is the use of the color red in the story. Red is considered to be the color of luck in Chinese tradition, and can be found on many New Year decorations and good luck charms. Although it is initially present to an almost overwhelming degree, to be found in the fireworks, the grandmother's clothing and the little girl's pajamas in order to emphasize the festive occasion and the hope for good fortune in the coming year (see Fig. 7), Huang weaves the symbolic color more subtly weaves into subsequent illustrations.

Fig. 7. The Little Girl and Grandmother; Zhong-Yang Huang,
from David Bouchard, *The Dragon New Year* 3.

The story begins with a little Chinese girl who is frightened by the multitude of noises and colors from the Lunar New Year celebrations filtering into her room. Against a backdrop of exploding fireworks and shouting, she begs her grandmother to stay with her and explain what is happening.[212] Her fear seems to be only partially real — each year, her grandmother tells her the same story to lull her to sleep, so the little girl is at least partly pretending in order to hear the tale again. The illustration supports this, as the girl is shown clapping her hands over her ears, burrowing into her grandmother's arms, but not looking truly afraid. Tolerantly, the old woman agrees to retell the story, the mysterious beginning of the New Year celebration. With the brief introduction, the narrative turns to the story within

212 Bouchard 4.

the story, set hundreds of years in the past. Although the text is still written in the grandmother's voice, neither she nor the safe, modern bedroom are present any longer, allowing the reader to travel to a different time: "Had we been here before, in the olden days, when there were no such loud sounds or bright lights,... Had we been here then, we would have found... Our village so deathly quiet that at midday we could count the mice by the ticking of their tiny nails on the vacant cobblestone streets."[213] In this time, the people live in fear of a ferocious dragon named New Year, who resides in the sea and appears each year to feast on its hapless victims. The villagers have no choice but to flee into the mountains, waiting for the dragon to vanish once more. During this part of the story, the color red is almost entirely absent from the illustrations, which are kept in shades of blue-gray and sandy brown. The only time it appears is as a small, diamond-shaped design on a vase, bearing the Hànzì for "spring."[214] However, the flower arrangement in the vase is wilted, as devoid of life as the village in the background, a symbol for hopelessness.

At the time of the dragon's reappearance, a young fisherman remains at sea to secure his nets, and is caught in New Year's whirlpool as it emerges from the sea.[215] Crouched on top of a tidal wave, the dragon waits for a moment before swooping in to devour the fisherman. The entire scene is witnessed by the young man's mother, who can do nothing but stand by and watch as her son dies and the dragon disappears back into the sea.[216] The pages depicting the fisherman's demise are the only ones in the book apart from the villagers' exodus that cover an entire double-page each, with the text embedded in a small, washed-out box to the upper or lower right. As mentioned above, this is used to depict the totality of the roaring sea and the dragon that commands its waves. Here, too, the color red is used, but again, it is concentrated in a single spot, namely the sash and loincloth worn by the young fisherman whose luck has left him.

213 Bouchard 7.

214 Bouchard 6.

215 Bouchard 11.

216 Bouchard 15.

Heartbroken over her son's death, his old mother decides to stay behind the next year despite the villagers' pleas. She wants to await death in the village, as she has nothing left to live for.[217] As night falls, she receives an unexpected visitor. The stranger is none other than Buddha, who asks the woman for food and shelter. She welcomes him into her home, but warns him of the imminent coming of the dragon. Buddha, however, has appeared to help her and tells her how to fight New Year: "Listen carefully! This dragon is a sea dragon. It does not know fire! This dragon's home is muffled by the sea. It knows nothing of loud sound! Let us create for it a welcome it will not soon forget!"[218] He orders the old woman to prepare their meal outdoors and lights a large bonfire in the village square as she chops and pounds on the food with all her strength. Soon, the dragon appears from the sea and moves to attack them, yet it is confused by the sight of the raging bonfire, which, miraculously, has taken on the shape of the dead fisherman.[219] Frightened by the noise and fire, the dragon recoils as the ghost of the fisherman tosses a net of fiery sparks, capturing the dragon and hurling it back into the waves.[220] In these scenes, the color red is naturally very prominent because of the blazing fire, symbolizing the triumph of good fortune over disaster. After the dragon's defeat, Buddha praises the old woman's courage and kindness, and advises her, "You have prepared the way for better and safer years to come. Share this gift as you will."[221] This marks the end of the tale and the return to the present day, where the little girl has finally fallen into a peaceful sleep. The grandmother is depicted as covering her with a red-hued blanket, content in the knowledge that she has shared an important story with her grandchild, "a story that this child would someday share with her own granddaughter."[222]

---

217 Bouchard 17.

218 Bouchard 17.

219 Bouchard 20.

220 Bouchard 24-26.

221 Bouchard 27.

222 Bouchard 29-30.

4.9. *Naomi's Tree*

Joy Kogawa's book is an adaptation of her novel *Obasan*, one of the most prominent works of Japanese Canadian literature. The children's version tells the story of a Japanese cherry tree as it travels the long way to Canada in the form of a cherry seed, is planted in the backyard of a young couple's house and grows to become a dear friend to Naomi, the household's youngest grandchild and the protagonist of *Obasan*. *Naomi's Tree* weaves two different narrative perspectives together, namely that of the cherry tree and of Naomi, as they are forced to part, yet still longingly think of each other. The text is accompanied by Ruth Ohi's full-page watercolor and charcoal illustrations. Although the charcoal is used to sketch the line art, the colors are allowed to blend and blur together, creating very soft, fleeting images. They very much suit the story in this respect, as the overall narrative tone is one of bitter-sweetness, reminiscent of the concept of *mono no aware* — a poignant realization of loss and the ephemeral.

The story begins with an explanation of the origin and meaning of the cherry tree, which is particularly tied to Japanese culture. The custom of *hanami*, or "flower-viewing," inspires thousands of Japanese to visit the parks and watch the cherry blossoms each year. "The Maker, who had created the world for friendship, smiled upon the cherry tree and blessed it," Kogawa writes, "So it was that, over time, the beautiful tree became known as the Friendship Tree."[223] As seen in Fig. 8, Ohi's choice of coloring and perspective foreground the cherry tree as the most important part of the illustrations, a vibrant swirl of pink hues scattering its petals across the celebrating people. The almost complete lack of charcoal outline gives the blossoms an added feeling of softness, matching the symbolic nature of the cherry tree — love, beauty, and transience.[224]

---

223 Joy Kogawa, *Naomi's Tree* (Markham: Fitzhenry & Whiteside, 2008) 3-4.

224 Khoon Choy Lee, *Japan — Between Myth and Reality* (Singapore: World Scientific, 1995) 142.

Fig. 8. Naomi and Her Family: Ruth Ohi,
from Joy Kogawa, *Naomi's Tree*, 9.

However, the narrative soon focuses on the fate of a particular tree — a small cherry seed hidden away in the sleeve of a young bride as she leaves for Canada with her husband.[225] The couple decide to plant the seed in the backyard of their new home, where it grows into a strong tree just as the family itself grows with children, and eventually, two grandchildren. Naomi and her older brother Stephen spend much time in the shade of the tree. Naomi in particular comes to consider the cherry tree a friend, clambering among its branches and singing songs.[226] Yet her cheerful, carefree childhood is over all too soon — one day, Naomi's mother abruptly leaves the family to return to Japan and care for her sick grandmother. Although she

225 Kogawa 6.

226 Kogawa 8.

promises to return, she never does, as the Second World War breaks out and prevents her from leaving the country. The illustration is almost entirely dominated by the mother's sad face, her figure darkened and dressed in dark clothes, symbolizing not only the pain of departure but also the fate that awaits her. Notably, Naomi is depicted standing in the background, small and worried, wearing a dress the same color as the cherry blossoms, thus adding to the impression of fleetingness. The changes do not stop here, however. Naomi is forced to leave the house together with her father and brother to work in an internment camp, although Kogawa glosses over this part of the story.[227] Before she has to leave, Naomi hugs her favorite tree, which trembles in sadness, its rustling branches whispering words of parting.

The narrative then skips ahead to the end of the war, choosing to focus on Naomi's relationship with the cherry tree rather than her experience in the Japanese internment camp, although the accompanying illustration shows her working the fields at a slightly older age. Her mother is dead and she can return neither to her old home nor to her carefree days. As the years go by, she slowly begins to forget about the house and her favorite tree.[228] The tree, however, does not stop thinking about her, even though other people move into the family's former home. It sings its prayers for Naomi's safety, "May she be safe. May she be kind. May she come back again,"[229] and is answered by the insects miles and miles away, which reassure it that Naomi is safe and will, indeed, return one day. The accompanying image shows the cherry tree bare and covered in snow, a lonely being that almost appears to stretch in the direction in which Naomi has gone.[230]

At this point, the story fast-forwards again to depict Naomi and Stephen as elderly people who finally return to visit their birthplace. Naomi fears that the house might have been destroyed, but it still stands, empty and abandoned. The siblings decide to enter, filled with a painful kind of nostalgia. In the backyard, they find the cherry tree, now ancient and injured, and as

227 Kogawa 12.

228 Kogawa 17.

229 Kogawa 18.

230 Kogawa 19.

Naomi puts her hand on its bark, she finally remembers the happy days of her early childhood. Unable to hold back her tears, she embraces the tree: "'Dear Cherry Tree,' she said softly. 'My dear, dear Cherry Tree. How old we have become."[231] Once again, there is an added nuance to be discovered in Ohi's art — Naomi is wearing a coat the color of cherry blossoms, although her silhouette is at first so dark that this is barely discernible. It is only when she rediscovers the cherry tree in the subsequent picture that the shadows fade away, revealing the color of her clothes, almost a metaphor for her journey towards a relief from pain.[232] By contrast, the cherry tree's dark trunk is the only part that is visible in this picture — although the memories she shares with the tree are dear to Naomi, confronting them is also painful. It is only in the next panel that the tree is shown in full, a few pink blossoms dotting its gnarled branches as it seemingly bends down to return Naomi's embrace, showing that there is sweetness and joy to be found among the pain.[233] During the embrace, Naomi also remembers her mother's promise to return, and whispers, "Are you there, Mama?"[234] against the tree. And suddenly, she can hear her mother's voice, answering softly from within, "Yes, my dear Naomi. You are safe with me. You are at home with me."[235] Her mother's soul lingers with the tree, a fitting representation of the cherry tree's connection to both life and death in Japanese folklore. Naomi beckons Stephen to listen, as well, both allowing themselves to be soothed by the voices of their mother and the tree. The story ends with the cherry tree's prayer, as it entreats the world to be a safe, kind place.

---

231 Kogawa 22.

232 Kogawa 23.

233 Kogawa 25.

234 Kogawa 24.

235 Kogawa 24.

4.10. *Neekna and Chemai*

Jeannette Armstrong's children's book tells the story of two little girls belonging to the Okanagan First Nations people, Neekna and Chemai. Through their eyes, the author portrays the daily life of the tribe — their work, their games, their stories and their traditions — in a time long before the influence of the European settlers was felt across the land.

Neekna and Chemai does not follow a plot in the traditional sense. Instead, the book is split into sections according to the four seasons, detailing the activities as perceived by Neekna, the first person narrator, and to a lesser extent, by her best friend Chemai. The story is accompanied by Okanagan artist Barbara Marchand's watercolor and ink illustrations. Fig. 9 represents the color scheme of the whole book, which primarily consists of hues of blue, yellow and brown. Only rarely does a spot of green or pale red enter the picture. Most of the illustrations feature animal or plant silhouettes in the background, sometimes even a spirit or legendary figure, to illustrate the Okanagans' connection to nature. All the human characters depicted are rather iconic with very few distinctive features, as only Neekna's family members are not reduced to silhouettes, and it is only possible to tell Neekna and her friend Chemai apart from the context of the story (see Fig. 9). The characters are depicted wearing the traditional Okanagan clothing — long dresses made from animal hide and fez-shaped caps for the women, leggings, shirts and headbands for the men.[236] It should also be noted that the placement of the images and the typesetting are not ideal — at times, the text at least partly covers the illustrations, leading to visibility problems since the opacity of the pictures has not been adjusted to accommodate the writing.

---

236 "Lifestyle of the Okanagan," *Osoyoos Museum*, 19 May 2009, 11 Dec. 2009 <http://osoyoosmuseum.ca/lifestyle_of_the_okanagan.htm>.

Fig. 9. Hair-Braiding; Barbara Marchand,
from Jeanette C. Armstrong, *Neekna and Chemai* 39.

The book begins in winter, and gradually moves forward through the year, ending with autumn. Each chapter revolves around the various tasks the season permits or requires, such as gathering food, making tools, or moving the camp to a different location. Neekna and Chemai are too young to be heavily involved in the work, so they have more time to play than the older children, yet they still receive instructions that will prepare them for the time when they will become old enough to be full-fledged members of the tribe. The seasonal chapters also contain at least one Okanagan legend each, usually told by Neekna's great-grandmother, whom she calls "Tupa," or the village chief, to pass their cultural heritage on to the children and teach them to respect the things they encounter every day. A lot of information about the two central characters is either only implied or left to the imagination — although the story revolves around their lives, it does not revolve around them per se. They are depicted as fun-loving and carefree, obedient to their parents and grandparents, and eager to discover the world. For the most part, however, the narrative focuses on describing the various happenings in the village rather than on developing the characters.

The winter chapter starts with Neekna ushering Chemai out of bed to show her the fresh snowfall. The family eats breakfast in their underground lodge, traditional winter quarters for the Okanagan people which were dug in the ground to conserve heat and which one could enter through the roof.[237] During the meal, each family member announces what they are planning to do during the day. These parts are rendered in the highly didactic style that permeates not just the narrative of the book, but the dialogue, as well:

> My father said, "Today my sons will track rabbits and make snares. I will show them where to put them. Tonight we will eat roast rabbit." My mother nodded and said, "Today my mother and daughters will work in the big house. We will finish weaving the mats and bags that we need for the hop dance." My grandpa said, "Today I will continue my teaching of the older boys. We will make more spears and arrow tips. It is hard work, but we will need many for hunting this summer."[238]

This listing shows the traditional hierarchy and division of labor — the women were in charge of teaching the girls and had duties that mainly concerned themselves with the gathering of food and maintaining the home, while the men were in charge of instructing the boys, hunting, and the crafting of weapons. Generally, the entire family, including grandparents, aunts and uncles, was involved in bringing up the children.[239] Neekna and Chemai watch the women and older girls as they work on sewing clothes, weaving mats and tanning hides, but eventually decide to play with the other young children.[240] In their play-tipi, they are visited by Neekna's great-grandmother, who has come to teach them about various aspects of life. She explains that winter is the time for the Okanagan people to prepare for the coming year, not just in terms of crafting tools and items, but also in terms of spirituality. During the winter dances, the people pray for lots of

237 "Lifestyle of the Okanagan."

238 Armstrong 4.

239 "Lifestyle of the Okanagan."

240 Armstrong 5.

snow to keep the earth moist in spring, which will make for a rich harvest. She warns the children to adhere to the traditions as ordained by the Great Spirit, lest misfortune befall the entire land.[241] The pictures show the great-grandmother gesturing dramatically as the girls listen eagerly, bright smiles on their faces despite the serious mood. Afterwards, she tells them another story about a little boy who foolishly challenges the North Wind by not wearing proper clothes in winter. He loses his way in a snow storm, but the North Wind allows him to return home with the promise of worse punishment should he not learn his lesson.[242]

The chapter of spring opens with an illustration bathed in yellow, a contrast to the mainly blue-gray toned pictures of winter. It depicts the children standing around a small patch of buttercups, the bright rays of the sun streaming down from the sky. In fact, they almost seem to be wafting and curling like smoke, which could also make them a spiritual representation.[243] Spring is the time for gathering plants and roots. The girls are instructed by Neekna's grandmother to look for a specific plant that will help them prepare their stomachs for fresh food after the long period of eating nothing but dried goods. The children are enthusiastic about helping to gather plants, an activity in which the entire tribe participates. Later, they decide to move the camp to a different location in order to dig for bitterroots. Abandoning the underground huts, they pack the mats they have woven during winter in order to be able to erect the typical mat lodges of the region during the warmer months.[244] The children watch as the adults get ready to leave, bundling up all the things they have made during the winter and loading them on horses. The long trek is made on foot, only the old people ride on horseback.[245] As they dig for roots, the great-grandmother tells them another story: the legend of Chief Bitterroot, who gave up his

241 Armstrong 8-10.

242 Armstrong 10-12.

243 Armstrong 13.

244 Dorothy Kennedy, and Randy Bouchard. "Native People: Plateau." *The Canadian Encyclopedia*. 2009. Historica Foundation. 4 Dec. 2009 <http://www.thecanadian encyclopedia.com/index.cfm?PgNm=TCE&Params=A1ARTA0009071>.

245 Armstrong 19.

own body to become food to the people of future generations. To honor him, the Okanagan hold a feast on the first day of digging for roots.[246]

Summer is the season to pick the ripe fruit, especially berries. The chapter begins with the tribe relocating once more to gather Saskatoon berries, presumably to make pemmican, a dish of meat and berries that was used as rations on travels.[247] During the meal, the chief makes a speech, reminding the people to honor Chief Saskatoon Berry, who also donated his body as food with the help of the Great Spirit. The berry months continue as Neekna and Chemai accompany Neekna's mother to pick blackberries high up in the mountains. It is the first time the children are allowed to go on horseback, hanging on tightly to the adult rider's belt, as none of the horses depicted are bearing a saddle.[248] The mother uses the gathered berries to make a dish of cooked, mashed berries, causing Neekna to remark that she likes summer best of all seasons because of the fresh food and the warm sun. It should be noted here that the illustration on this page does not correspond to the text — Neekna explains that her father catches trout and that she and Chemai chase after ducks, yet the illustration depicts a dead fish floating upside down in the water, along with a cluster of black birds that vaguely resemble crows.

The last chapter revolves around autumn, thereby concluding the seasonal cycle. The tribe moves to the waterfalls in Okanagan Valley to catch salmon. The Okanagan Falls were the main fishing spot for the First Nations living in the area, where they would set up weirs to catch the fish to dry it in large quantities as preparation for the coming winter.[249] Between pages 31 to 33 occurs a typesetting error: from one page to the next, the narrative flow is broken by a paragraph that is neither related to the previous nor the following passage. The entirety of page 32 is a segment missing from an earlier part of the story — the arrival of the great-grandmother at the children's play-tipi in the very first chapter on page 8. On page 33, the narrative

246 Armstrong 20-21.

247 "Pemmican," *Encyclopædia Britannica Online*, 2009, Encyclopædia Britannica, 11 Dec. 2009 <http://www.britannica.com/EBchecked/topic/449526/pemmican>.

248 Armstrong 26-27.

249 "Lifestyle of the Okanagan."

continuity is restored. The chief orders the catch to be divided equally among the entire tribe. Neekna and Chemai help to hang the slices of salmon on the drying racks, with the accompanying illustration showing the fish lined up on poles in their traditional, vaguely triangular shape. On the way back to the winter camp, they pass a large free-standing rock formation which the grandmother identifies as "Rock Woman."[250] She explains that this formation is a landmark for travelers who leave sacrificial gifts to receive divine protection in return. According to legend, she was once a human who was changed into a rock to guard the Okanagan valley. Neekna is greatly impressed by the story and expresses her hope that future generations will also honor the Rock Woman in the same way.[251] The last part of the chapter focuses on a big feast in the village as the hunters return from a successful hunt. One thing worthy of note is that the illustrations show Neekna and Chemai wearing braids from this point on. Neekna's mother is shown braiding their hair, worn loose until then, in the same style as all the adults and older children wear it — parted in the middle, twin braids falling past their shoulders. It appears that this signifies the children's acceptance as fully-fledged members of the tribe, which is also supported by the subsequent narrative passage. The chief makes a long speech about his people's way of life, admonishing them to always honor their ancestors, as well as the animals and plants that are part of their lives. He cautions that forgetting these cornerstones of their beliefs will lead to wanton destruction, and instructs the people to pass these teachings on to their grandchildren.[252] When Neekna is impatient to begin eating, her grandmother scolds her by reiterating the chief's teachings in slightly different words. She tells the girl to hold up her bowl of food and think about the gifts given to her. As Neekna follows the instructions, she begins to realize why all the women who are so important in her life — her mother, grandmother and great-grandmother — are so wise: they live by the ways they were taught by their mothers and grandmothers, and Neekna resolves to teach her future children the same.

---

250 Armstrong 36-37.

251 Armstrong 37.

252 Armstrong 40.

5. Comparative Analysis

Having previously summarized and analyzed the books one at a time, this chapter will focus on the uncovering and analysis of common themes. As the selected books treat a wide variety of topics in a number of different ways, the themes discussed below will naturally not be present in every book — nevertheless, very different books will sometimes yield unexpected parallels. In addition, it must be said that the analysis purposely focuses on a limited number of themes. Multicultural and regional children's picturebooks present a veritable wellspring of layers, themes and angles that could be examined, but to discuss each and every one would simply go beyond the scope of this thesis. Therefore, this chapter will begin with a comparative analysis of the various child protagonists, loosely based on Sorin and Galloway's constructs of childhood (see page 17), followed by a comparison of immigrant narratives, the use of animal figures to treat complex abstract topics such as freedom or reincarnation, the preservation of cultural heritage in writing, degrees of westernization in narratives centering on First Nations cultures, and the treatment of historical events in some of the narratives.

5.1. Representations of Childhood

As stated above, this section will take a look at the child protagonists in the selected books by examining them within the framework of childhood constructs proposed in Sorin and Galloway. However, due to the limited scope and sample material, only four of these ten categories will find application in the analysis. In addition, a new category has been added in order to facilitate the analysis of children's books with no distinct individuals as protagonists.

5.1.1. The Innocent Child

In many ways, McFarlane's *Waiting for the Whales* presents the protagonist, an unnamed little girl, as the epitome of what Sorin and Galloway refer to as "the innocent child." This construct views the child as carefree, inherently good, naïve or even ignorant, and very vulnerable. By contrast, the adult assumes the role of a powerful protector, who lovingly nurtures the child yet only exposes it to influences and environments the adult deems suitable.[253] Such is the underlying situation in *Waiting for the Whales* — the little girl exists in a protective, nurturing sphere crafted for her by her mother and grandfather. The hut by the sea is her entire world, and in it, she seems to enjoy boundless freedom. She can be as serious, stubborn or wild[254] as she likes, since the adults appear to accept this as a part of her personality. Her grandfather is responsible for teaching her how to care for the garden and to survive in the woods, always by her side to instruct and guide her. When he becomes too old to work and wander extensively, the mother assumes the position of teacher and guardian. "Froebel's metaphor of *kindergarten*, the 'garden of children,' positions children as seedlings, in a state of natural goodness, to be cared for and nurtured as they blossom into adults,"[255] Sorin writes in "Changing Images of Childhood," a concept that also works in the context of McFarlane's story. Just as she is helping to raise the planted crops, the little girl is also a 'seedling' in a garden, one her mother and grandfather have carefully prepared for her. They are the center of her world, to the point where they appear to be the *only* people in it — as stated previously, the absolute lack of hints concerning any outside influence, be it friends of the same age, teachers, neighbors or acquaintances from town, anyone else besides the mother and grandfather who might have contact with the little girl, make it doubtful that such people even exist in her world. The hut, the beach, and the surrounding woods appear to have been specifically selected as a sphere in which the little girl can spend an idyllic childhood, in which she can explore the world yet feel secure, and always have a guardian figure to turn to. Given the idea that her mother might be fleeing an abusive relationship, something that is supported by the fact that she appears unannounced with her entire belongings packed, seeking to reconnect with her estranged father, one can easily hypothesize why

253 Reesa Sorin, and G. Galloway, "Construct of Childhood: Constructs of Self," *Children Australia* 31.2 (2006): 21.

254 McFarlane 16.

255 Sorin 13.

she might wish for her daughter to maintain her innocence and not experience any hurt.

5.1.2. The Savior Child

According to Sorin and Galloway, the noble child, or savior child, is charged with supporting or even saving others, often at the cost of its own needs. In this power relationship, the child tends to assume its position as savior through specific circumstances because the adults in its environment either do not or cannot master certain adult challenges. Therefore, it is up to the child to act because the adults depend on it.[256] To a degree, such a constellation can be observed in Wallace's *Duncan's Way*. Duncan's family is in a precarious position, as the father has lost his job as a fisherman, and the mother cannot support them by herself. The father has fallen into a depression, withdrawing from his family and unable to muster enough energy to act. Duncan's mother is overworked and overburdened, helpless in the face of her husband's depression, resigned to the fact that their savings will eventually dwindle into nothing and they will have to leave all they know behind. Even Duncan's brother Luke, who appears to be a few years older, is unable to think of a way out. Duncan himself is constantly rebuffed when he tries to address the family's problems, as his attempts to cheer up his father fail, and his mother reacts hotly when Duncan acutely pinpoints the source of his father's illness. Rejected and confused, he only finds a patient listener in Mr. Marshall, a retired fisherman, who helps to nudge Duncan towards a solution, namely the transformation of the family fishing boat into a mobile bakery. Duncan presents his plan so thoughtfully and concretely that its feasibility cannot be ignored by his family. In this manner, Duncan manages to save his family in more ways than one. They are not only able to stay in their beloved hometown, but the harmony is restored, as the father recovers and the family are able to assume their conventional roles once more: the parents in command of the ship and its onboard kitchen, while the children return to be contributors rather than leaders.

256 Sorin and Galloway 21.

5.1.3. The Victimized Child

The child as a victim finds itself in circumstances utterly beyond its control. Unable to handle the situation, the child is swept along by the events like driftwood, as the adults are either powerless themselves or absent from the child's life, either literally or metaphorically. Sorin cites war, famine, or poverty as examples,[257] but there are many situations where children are deprived of both control and security, such as family break-ups, or moving to a different country. The protagonists of *Courage to Fly* (Meg) and *The Chinese Violin* (Lin Lin) both fall into this category, as well as Gita from *A Gift for Gita* and Naomi from *Naomi's Tree*. Lin Lin in particular is deprived of any kind of agency and power, as she is struggling not just to cope with her foreign environment, but also with the language barrier, her father's unemployment, and racist attacks against them. Although her father tries to be supportive of her, he, too, is mostly powerless and even has to resort to using his child to earn money by taking her along on his street performances. Neither of them are able to regain power on their own — it is by mere chance that Lin Lin's father manages to find employment, which also unburdens his young daughter a little. Lin Lin remains vulnerable throughout the story, as much of her happiness is tied to her father's happiness, and later on, to the violin she receives as a gift, which finally gives Lin Lin a method of communicating with the outside world and also a first measure of self-confidence. Meg's situation is similar, though she is at least not confronted with a language barrier and parental unemployment. Immigrating to a large city in Canada has disrupted her routine and stability. Her parents are almost entirely absent from both the narrative and her life; it is never established whether they have even realized their daughter's plight and simply do not know how to resolve it, or whether they have given up trying. Hence, Meg is not just powerless due to her circumstances, but also deprived of people she can turn to in order to comprehend and master her own problems. It is — again by mere chance — that she meets the old man who is able to read her like an open book and can thus provide her with advice and encouragement. Alone, Meg is unable to break free of her self-imposed imprisonment, but with the old man's help, she slowly begins to

---

257 Sorin 18.

perceive the world around her as something other than threatening, which eventually allows her to cast off her fears and make a new friend with whom she can face the world. *A Gift for Gita* provides a slightly different situation: Gita is part of a stable, loving middle-class family who have already adapted to their new life in Canada. However, that stability is tenuous, since the job offer her father receives creates an impromptu crisis within the family. In this crisis, where the family is faced with the difficult choice of remaining in Canada or returning to their home country of India, Gita is left entirely alone to struggle with her feelings on the matter. *Naomi's Tree* also places the child protagonist Naomi and her older brother Stephen into a situation where they are completely powerless. First, they are deprived of their mother, who returns to Japan to care for her sick grandmother, and is eventually killed during the Second World War. Naomi and her brother, together with many other Japanese Canadians, are forced to leave their homes and are deported to internment camps. As Naomi is powerless throughout her childhood, it is only when she has become an old woman that she is able to comprehend the events and obtain some kind of closure by visiting her old family home again. In each case, the abandonment and lack of parental protection might have several reasons. For one, no matter how much they might try, parents are not omnipotent. Tumultuous or traumatic events can affect them deeply and render them almost or entirely helpless, which, in turn, might cause them to involuntarily neglect their children. For another, it is possible for them not to understand their children's needs, and since children are often unable to communicate their needs with the same insight and directness as adults, these needs may remain unnoticed or misunderstood. For a third, the lack of parental involvement in *Courage to Fly* and *A Gift for Gita* actually contributes to the protagonists' growth, who begin to discover their own strength and ability to think about their situation. This can be a positive message to young readers, an encouragement to discover their own abilities and hidden strengths.

5.1.4. The Agentic Child

The agentic child is described as a social actor, who is capable of participating in the shaping of its life and education. Rather than being forced into a role that grants it too much or too little power, the child is allowed to co-construct its life together with adults. The adults both give and receive help by lending their knowledge and power rather than imposing it.[258] Solomon in *Solomon's Tree* is such a child, since he is allowed to choose his own pastimes and make his own discoveries. Solomon explores his favorite maple tree on his own, finding the birds' nests, the butterfly larvae, and countless other small wonders, which is a contrast to the little girl in *Waiting for the Whales*, who is constantly guided and instructed by her grandfather. However, Solomon is not alone — his family is able to recognize his grief over the loss of his tree and offers to help him meet his tree again in a changed form. It is Solomon's choice to agree with the proposal, and it is also his choice to join in the ritual dance at the beginning, where he sings his own song rather than repeating his uncle's words. Although the uncle, as the master craftsman, does the majority of the difficult work, he does so in accordance with the information Solomon gives him, and teaches the boy to perform certain tasks himself. In return, he receives Solomon's interest and enthusiasm, which makes it likely that Solomon will internalize these traditions or even wish to become an apprentice in the craft one day.

5.1.5. The Child as a Story Agent

This category is not to be confused with the agentic child. It has been added in order to aid the analysis of children's books with no distinct protagonists. Not a power constellation per se, it is meant to describe books where neither child nor adult figures are distinguishable as individuals, or round characters, and are instead depicted as nearly interchangeable parts of a collective or community. This is the case in Armstrong's *Neekna and Chemai*, wherein the protagonists are identified by name but seem completely identical even though they are not twins or even related. They have no distinct characteristics of their own, no preferences or dislikes, fears or hopes, and

258 Sorin 18.

instead act as "agents" driving the narrative forward; they exist to point out specific objects or features, such as plants or animals, showcase certain tasks and activities such as food-gathering or weaving, and ask questions concerning traditions or legends. Neither do the adults appear as individuals; rather, they are a collective personification of "the teacher," there to share their knowledge at certain points in the story and instruct the children. A similar collective can be observed in Kusugak's *Baseball Bats for Christmas*. The children are depicted as cheerful, mischievous and curious, and are generally seen playing, exploring or getting in trouble as a group. Arvaarluk's distinguishing feature is that he is asthmatic, but apart from this, he behaves just like the other children and cannot be readily identified in group illustrations. This also applies to the adults in the story — save for Father Didier and Rocky Parsons, who stand out simply because of their ethnicity and role within the community, none of the adults can be distinguished in the illustrations, and Arvaarluk's mother, though she makes a brief appearance, does not possess particular individuality. She functions as the "scolding parent" to threaten the children for misdemeanor, but little beyond that. In Kusugak's book, the event, namely the arrival of Christmas trees and the Inuit children's collective reactions take precedence over the characters' individuality. The narratives are not psychological problem narratives, and as such, do not delve deeply into the inner worlds of the characters involved. Moreover, in Kusugak's book, one could say that the humorous, almost satirical presentation of the culture clash is facilitated through a child narrator's point of view. 'Out of the mouth of babes, oft times come gems,' goes the old saying, and in *Baseball Bats for Christmas*, the children's lack of knowledge and single-minded pursuit of fun enables the ridicule of missionary and homogenization efforts in a small, isolated Inuit community.

Similarly the characters in Bouchard's *The Dragon New Year* exist to drive the story forward. They do not partake in the story itself, but exist as part of a frame narrative in order to both provide a point of identification for a young audience. The little Chinese girl in *The Dragon New Year* has almost no individual characteristics — her role is to motivate the telling of a classical bedtime story by begging her grandmother to do so under the pretense of being afraid of the fireworks. Likewise, the grandmother character fulfills the role of the storyteller, the parental figure who will indulge the child's begging and share a story before it is time to sleep, but she does not possess particular individuality.

5.2. The Immigrant Experience

As Canada is a multicultural society with a high rate of immigration, many children's books pick the experience of immigration from the child's perspective as a central theme. Bewilderment, isolation, homesickness, feeling overwhelmed and being treated as "other" are common themes. The stories maintain a hopeful tone, however. Despite the fact that the characters' fate is a difficult one, they manage to persevere and are able to regain a measure of control over their lives in the end. Immigrant children can find their own difficulties reflected and discussed in the text, and may take away strategies to overcome these difficulties. Although they might not know what it means to leave one's homeland and emigrate to a completely different country, non-immigrant children may still find these texts accessible — they themselves might have been forced into situations that are comparable to a degree, such as moving to a different city, or they might remember their own first few days in a new school, filled with uncertainty and awkwardness. Therefore, such narratives might appeal to their understanding and tolerance. Moreover, the books try to present Canada in a positive light, a country welcoming to all immigrants despite the initial difficulties they may encounter. First impressions might be disorienting at best and negative at worst, yet the country does have positive experiences to offer, even if it takes time to discover them. This kind of presentation might help immigrant children to integrate, but, true to Canadian multiculturalism policy, allow them keep a degree of their own culture and practices. The child ought not substitute Canada for its home country, but find a balance between the two.

Among the selected works, Gilmore's *A Gift for Gita*, Harrison's *Courage to Fly* and Thien's *The Chinese Violin* concentrate on the topic of immigration and immigration-related problems of children from different cultural backgrounds. The characters portrayed in these works come from three of the current largest immigrant groups[259] — Rachna Gilmore's book deals with an Indian family, Troon Harrison tells the story of a girl from a Caribbean background, and Madeleine Thien details the experiences of a Chinese father and daughter. Despite their shared fate, one difference between the central characters immediately becomes apparent. Gita and Meg hail from countries with a colonial history where English is spoken by a significant percentage of the population; in other words, both protagonists have a reasonably good command of the language and can communicate with other people in Canada. In contrast to this stands Thien's protagonist Lin Lin, a girl from an unspecified region in rural China, where the English language is neither part of the school curriculum nor part of daily life. It is interesting, then, that Meg, the Caribbean girl, and Lin Lin are suffering from a similar case of muteness in the foreign country. Both protagonists are newly arrived in Canada, feeling overwhelmed and frightened, and subsequently become feeble and isolated. However, their reasons are fundamentally different. For Lin Lin, the culture shock is much more severe — from a small country town, a place where she knew everyone and could speak to them, she is catapulted into the foreign metropolis of Vancouver, the noise of vehicles and voices sweeping over her "like an ocean."[260] And, similar to the rushing sound of ocean waves, she only hears white noise. At school, she is isolated because she cannot understand the lessons or the other children, and is thus always left by herself. Meg's situation is different. She has some experience with Western culture and an even better command of English than her mother, who speaks with a strong accent,[261] yet she is seized by a kind of agoraphobia that Lin Lin does not share, although she harbors similar feelings of being lost and swamped with foreign sounds and impressions. Meg is capable of communicating with people outside her family, yet her insurmountable terror renders her speechless and isolated. Harrison never gives precise reasons for Meg's fear other than the strange sights and sounds of the bustling city, leaving the impression that her muteness is self-generated and self-perpetuating. By contrast, Lin Lin has her father with

259 Statistics Canada. *Population by Selected Ethnic Origins, by Province and Territory (2006 Census).*

260 Thien 8.

261 Harrison 13.

whom she can share her worries, but Meg seems unable to do even this. As previously stated, Harrison does not detail why Meg's family leaves her to her own devices. Although the end result — beginning acceptance and self-confidence — is the same, the sources of Lin Lin's and Meg's strength are different. Lin Lin's focal figure is definitely her father, to whom she feels very close. Through his support and hard work, Lin Lin is eventually able to select the Chinese violin as her way of communicating with the outside world and overcoming her nervousness and loneliness. In Meg's case, her family is present yet so absent from her troubles that the help she so sorely needs has to come from the outside world, via the old man's kind-hearted advice. His slightly cryptic words are what allows Meg to make the decision to conquer her fears.

A Gift for Gita focuses on a different aspect of an immigrant child's experience, namely the feeling of being torn between two cultures, the old country and the new. An important difference between this book and the former two is that Gita, its protagonist, has been living in Canada for quite some time already. Compared to Meg and Lin Lin, who have barely just begun to see the new country as a positive or at least not entirely negative entity, Gita has firmly settled in Canada. She and her family have "put down roots,"[262] as her father chooses to phrase it — Gita has managed to find a new best friend to whom she feels very close, she has grown used to the climate and enjoys partaking in new activities such as canoeing or ice-skating. She has begun to think of Canada as her home, contrary to Meg or Lin Lin, who cling to memories of their old home to comfort themselves in an environment which they perceive as unfriendly, if not downright hostile. Because Gita has taken the next steps and managed to build a home for herself in Canada, her grandmother's visit and the subsequent announcement that the family might move back to India confuse her all the more. It is extremely difficult for her to decide where she wants to belong, as she has fond memories of both countries, in contrast to the other protagonists, who are barely able to adjust to life in Canada. The story forces Gita to come to terms with the fact that she has two homes, and that her physical location is not all that matters when it comes to belonging. What allows her to make that decision comparatively quickly is that her family and Gita herself have already

262 Gilmore 10.

merged parts of Canadian lifestyle with parts of their Indian identity — Gita speaks perfect English, yet affectionately refers to her grandmother as "Naniji," the Hindi address for one's maternal grandmother. Gita is shown wearing jeans and a sweater, yet enjoys wearing the colorful saris her grandmother bestows upon her and her Canadian friend as gifts.[263] She loves traditional Indian mango ice cream[264] alongside pizza,[265] likes playing with the nesting doll just as much as she enjoys Canadian sports. In that sense, Gita's story is less about her finding a new identity and more about realizing that her new identity has already subconsciously formed — she cannot recall the exact process, how or when it happened, when she stopped missing her home in India,[266] but now she has to come to terms with the result. In this sense, *A Gift for Gita* depicts a "successful" immigrant child, who has managed to combine the best of both worlds into a new whole.

5.3. Images of Canada

As already stated above, part of the aim of immigrant problem narratives is to show the host country's positive aspects. In the three selected narratives, this is accomplished in two different ways. The first is the depiction of natural beauty, which, by extension, represents the beauty of Canada as a country. The second is the figure of a friend or confidant — generally white — who acts as a representative of the Canadian people and their good qualities (see 3.1). The beauty of the Canadian landscape is, in fact, the very first thing that the newly arrived children Meg and Lin Lin notice. Although she is feeling overwhelmed by the noise and activity, Lin Lin's spirits instantly lift when she visits a seaside park together with her father. The double-spread illustration shows her standing on a fallen log, staring out at the ocean with her arms lifted high as birds are soaring through the air and waves are crashing against the shore. The entire picture is tinged with warm, earthen colors, showing a view of the entire bay — all manner of plants rising in the foreground, the cityscape and mountains rising in the

263 Gilmore 22.

264 Gilmore 4.

265 Gilmore 12.

266 Gilmore 12.

background.[267] Lin Lin seems joyful for the first time since her arrival in Canada, thanks to the beautiful landscape. In fact, this is because the park reminds her of home,[268] of her small village with its river, its birds and grassy hills.[269] The beauty of nature works as a universal concept here; the park at the shore of Vancouver and its splendor are enough to make Lin Lin recall her rural life, and establishing this link between her home and Canada, marks her first positive experience in the new country. Similarly, Meg's attention is also first captured by the beautiful Canadian autumn. Although she has presumably lived in the country a little longer than Lin Lin, she has always been too frightened to truly look around. She runs home from school, intimidated by the looming skyscrapers, and even when she is safely in her room, she is not really looking at the landscape, but simply watching the other children and envying them the ease with which they move about and play.[270] It is not until she meets the old man practicing tai-chi in a courtyard that she actually begins to stop and take notice. The old man's words make her feel understood and allow her to achieve a measure of calm — she notices the radiant autumn leaves for the first time and even goes so far as to pick some up to take home.[271] The gesture is quite symbolic, as Meg has turned her room into the single safe haven she knows. By gathering the leaves and bringing them into her sanctuary, she permits a small part of Canada to enter her isolated, near-hermetical sphere. Gita's story, though different from the previous two, relies even more heavily, and more obviously, on nature as a symbol for Canada. As stated before, nearly every illustration contains the signature maple leaves, most often as silhouettes peeking into the family living room. Gita even remarks upon this to her grandmother, stating that the trees are celebrating her visit.[272] The maples, it seems, are partaking in the joyful reunion, symbolic of Canada's hospitality and welcoming atmosphere. Later on in the narrative, they even

---

267 Thien 10-11.

268 Thien 10.

269 Thien 2-4.

270 Harrison 4.

271 Harrison 8.

272 Gilmore 2.

provide Gita with shelter when she runs outside to think,[273] and again, it seems as if the trees are not simply trees, but also a stand-in for the patient Canada which allows people to find themselves.

The figures of the Canadian friend and confidant are varied. Both *A Gift for Gita* and *Courage to Fly* involve the protagonist's friend, a girl presumably their age, who comes (or has come) to mean a lot to them. Gita's friend Amy is not physically present in the story, but Gita mentions her quite often. Amy is a very important part of her life, and the person to whom her thoughts turn first and foremost when she thinks of being forced to leave the country[274] or about why she stopped missing her home in India.[275] Her friendship with Amy has soothed her homesickness and allowed her to open herself to life in Canada. In Meg's case, the emphasis on forming a new friendship with a Canadian girl is even more pronounced. In fact, the neighbor's girl Jenny seems like the embodiment of a welcoming Canada, as she is depicted as outgoing, friendly, and trying to invite Meg out to play many times; in other words, she attempts to persuade her to embrace life in Canada, but is eventually thwarted by Meg's constant refusal.[276] However, she becomes important again later in the narrative, when Meg has made the decision to set the captured swallow free. In fact, Meg is the one who, in a sudden, unexplained burst of spontaneity, invites Jenny to join her, and although the girl is surprised, she immediately agrees, harboring no trace of resentment.[277] True to the Canadian values of kindness and the willingness to work hard,[278] she forgives Meg's initial rejection and once again asks to play with her, and this time, Meg finds the courage to agree. In contrast, *The Chinese Violin* focuses more strongly on the figure of the mentor than on the friend of the same age. In fact, Lin Lin's friends play a very marginal role — they appear suddenly and abruptly once Lin Lin begins to take her traditional violin to school, leaving the reader to wonder when exactly Lin

273 Gilmore 10.

274 Gilmore 8.

275 Gilmore 12.

276 Harrison 5.

277 Harrison 22.

278 Waterston 4.

Lin has begun to make friends, and the text makes no mention of their impact on Lin Lin's acclimation process. Her school teacher, on the other hand, is a more important figure. She is the only one who seems to realize that Lin Lin is struggling with the language, and makes a special effort to help her. The teacher's kind, motherly demeanor almost makes Lin Lin uncomfortable, as the illustration shows her flinching and ducking her head between her shoulders when the teacher attempts to put a calming hand on her back.[279] It also stands to reason that it might be the teacher who has organized Lin Lin's appearance in a school concert at the end of the story, as she is depicted cheering in the front row next to the girl's father and it is doubtful that Lin Lin, shy as she is, volunteered for the part.[280] In all likelihood, the teacher is Lin Lin's first positive acquaintance in Canada, since she is unable to communicate with her peers. As such, she stands in sharp contrast to the indifferent or hostile environment Lin Lin has experienced thus far, instead acting as a representative of the patient, understanding Canadian who encourages the immigrant child's talents and traditions. The old Chinese man in *Courage to Fly* fulfills a role that is slightly similar to that of the teacher in *The Chinese Violin*, as he guides and aids Meg with his advice, yet he also differs from the other characters discussed thus far. An immigrant himself, he is an example of someone who has kept his identity within Canadian society, calmly practicing tai-chi in the park. His cryptic advice to Meg is also influenced by the philosophical principles of this particular school of tai-chi, as he uses the names of techniques from the Liuhebafa style to first point out Meg's problem to her, and later nudge her towards a solution.[281] Since many different cultures and philosophies have taken root in Canada, the old man can be seen as an aspect of this societal mosaic — present, visible, and able to solve difficulties with wholly different approaches. Yet at the same time, the air of a mystical sage who can discern with a glance the troubles of a girl he has never met before never quite leaves the old man, setting him apart from the other characters.

---

279 Thien 22.

280 Thien 31.

281 Harrison 31.

5.4. Remote Regions: Problems and Sanctuaries

Both *Waiting for the Whales* and *Duncan's Way* are set in remote, thinly populated areas of Canada where nature and its forces are much greater than the human beings who have settled there. *Waiting for the Whales* is set on the coast of British Columbia, whereas Ian Wallace's book unfolds in a small, unnamed town along the Newfoundland shore. Both settings inspire a sense of vastness and isolation in the reader, yet the situation of the characters in the respective stories is fundamentally different. The old man in McFarlane's story is living entirely alone, like a hermit in the "cedar-shingled cottage"[282] that he supposedly built himself. His existence is self-reliant — he grows his own crops, collects the spoils from the sea and gathers herbs in the forests. The only hint that there is even a village or town nearby is that the old man is said to sell what he cannot use himself.[283] Paradoxically, the old man is at once content and discontent with his life. He enjoys planting his garden and foraging in the woods; in fact, he seems to pride himself on his knowledge of the land: "He knew each tree, each clearing, each trail and where it led. He knew where to collect the best salal to send to florist shops in the city. He knew where to gather water-cress for his soups."[284] Yet he is also terribly lonely. Several times, the narrative speaks of his children who have moved away, and, or so it seems, left him behind — there is no mention of any kind of correspondence with them. The old man's only solace is watching the killer whales that appear in the bay each summer, and he laments their departure every time.[285] Yet it appears as if he has chosen isolation willingly — despite the fact that there is a town a way away, he continues to stay in his remote cottage, and does not seem to make any effort to contact his faraway family. His reasons are never explained, leaving the reader to speculate that something might have happened a long time ago, something that caused a rift between the old man and his children. As previously stated in chapter 4.1., the land is not a threatening element in the story — on the contrary, it is almost painted as

282 McFarlane 2.

283 McFarlane 4.

284 McFarlane 10.

285 McFarlane 4.

more secure than any concentration of civilization. The old man does not have to fear for his existence, and neither do his daughter and granddaughter — the land provides them with all they need, and what little they cannot produce themselves, they can obtain by selling the surplus they have. In the illustrations, the sea is always calm, stretching like a vast and gently swaying mirror. The only time winter storms are mentioned, the family's safety is not threatened; on the contrary, they sit at the window, clad in thick, warm pullovers, and are calmly watching the forces raging outside.[286] Their isolation means safety and untouchability, and nature appears as a benevolent friend who never fails to provide for them, a miracle to be admired.

Duncan's Way, on the other hand, paints a much harsher picture of life in remote regions. For one, the Newfoundland area is mostly bare — grass and rocks abound, lending it a forlorn appearance, and the sea regularly transports icebergs into the bay where Duncan and his family live, which hints at the cold, if not downright hostile climate. Duncan likes living there, unable to imagine leaving his home for any other part of Canada.[287] Yet, his existence and the existence of everyone else around him are threatened — not merely by the hostile climate, but by the fact that nature, in this barren place, is no longer able to provide for them. Their main source of income, the cod, is gone thanks to industrial overfishing, which puts all the small, regional fishermen out of business and deprives them of a means to sustain their livelihood for generations to come. The atmosphere created by the story is one of desolation, an empty land bordered by an empty sea. Here, the isolation is life-threatening, in direct opposition to *Waiting for the Whales*, where it is painted as desirable, safe and secure like a cradle. In *Duncan's Way*, it appears as a prison, for with the fish gone from the waters, entire communities built around this natural resource are doomed to a slow death. In contrast to the old man, who has chosen to live out life as a recluse, the isolation of Duncan and his family is one that stems from the topography and demographic make-up of the region, and it is one that is only stable as long as the main source of income, the cod, is thriving. As such, the family in *Waiting for the Whales* is incredibly fortunate, as the climate at their location does not only enable them to have multiple sources of in-

286 McFarlane 26-27.

287 Wallace 16.

come — and plentiful sources, at that — but that they are also surrounded by a stable community, however much they might distance themselves from it. The people who buy their crops are unlikely to disappear any time soon, which ensures their continued access to all the items and services, such as hardware or medical attention, that they cannot produce or perform themselves. The ending to *Duncan's Way* might be a silver lining for the family — from the way Duncan is depicted cheerfully holding up the bread his father has baked, one can assume that their bakery boat has become a success[288] — yet what remains is the claustrophobic atmosphere. The family's existence might be ensured, yet the Newfoundland region as a whole will continue to feel the effects of the collapse and continue to depopulate.

5.5. Animal Symbolism

Animal stories have always played an important role in Canadian children's literature. Waterston points out that as far back as the 19th century, writers such as Sir Charles G. D. Roberts caught the popular imagination with animal tales in *The Watchers of the Trails* and *Children of the Wild*.[289] Now, in the late 20th and early 21st century, the figure of the animal is still used in Canadian children's fiction. In some realistic children's books, it moves from being a faithful companion or observed wonder to a symbolic figure, a sign. *Waiting for the Whales* and *Courage to Fly* both heavily draw on an animal figure as a symbol in order to convey the complex concepts of death and freedom. Setting the story along the coast of British Columbia, the author makes a point to include much of the local plant life and landscape, and chooses to center the story around the appearance of the killer whales. The whales are rendered as natural wonders in the story, the illustrations showing off their awe-inspiring sight as they leap straight from the waves. The human being is rendered insignificant in the face of their might, a tiny silhouette gazing from the top of a cliff, mesmerized.[290] The whales bring joy to the old man (and subsequently, his family), to a point where he appears to treat their arrival like a celebration, waiting in anticipation and

288 Wallace 32.

289 Waterston 93.

290 McFarlane 5.

longing. The whales make an appearance at turning points in the narrative — first to underscore the old man's loneliness. The whales work as a metaphor for his life because just as they arrive and depart each year, so the old man's family, his wife and children, have arrived and departed. The second turning point occurs when he begins to accept his daughter and grandchild back into his life.[291] It is a ritual he has observed for a very long time, yet it has also always been a lonely and very private enterprise. The last turning point occurs upon the old man's death and fully renders the whales as symbolic possessors of his heart. As a way to comfort her daughter for the loss of her grandfather, the mother assures her that "[her] grandfather's spirit has gone to leap and swim with the whales."[292] This not only cements the importance of the whales in the family's life, but also paves the way for the ending, for the little girl discovers a new calf swimming in the midst of the herd when it returns in summer.[293] The girl's joy appears to extend beyond the simple discovery of an adorable baby whale; in fact, it is much more likely that it seems she believes her mother's soothing words, and views the new life as the embodiment, or perhaps even reincarnation, of her grandfather's soul. This revelation is very similar to the belief of coastal First Nations. There, the religious significance of animals also extends to the concept of death and rebirth, not as punishment but as reward — for example, the Kwakiutl First Nation believes that land hunters would be reborn as wolves while sea hunters would be reborn as whales.[294] As such, the whales in McFarlane's story have become symbolic carriers of the old man's soul, giving hope for a continued existence not just after death, but on this Earth, in a concrete, physical form that is one with nature.

Courage to Fly stands in stark contrast to *Waiting for the Whales*. It employs the swallow as a symbol of freedom and courage, a small, fragile bird very unlike the majestic, untouchable whales. It is, of course, no accident

291 McFarlane 14-15.

292 McFarlane 23.

293 McFarlane 30.

294 Antonia Mills, "Reincarnation Belief among North American Indians and Inuit: Context, Distribution, and Variation," *Amerindian Rebirth — Reincarnation Belief among North American Indians and Inuit*, eds. Antonia Mills and Richard Slobodin (Toronto: Toronto UP, 1994) 34.

that Harrison picks the swallow for the purposes of her story. Since ancient times, the swallow has always been considered a bird of freedom. Several Bible translations use the term "swallow" to denote concepts of freedom, and although there is debate about whether or not these translations are correct, the fact remains that some translators considered the swallow the best representative of freedom.[295] As previously stated, birds in general are used as a metaphor for Meg's behavior — she, too, is small and easily frightened, urgently fluttering to the safety of her "nest." The metaphor is even supported by the illustrations; startled pigeons are present to echo her frantic dash home.[296] Yet it is not a pigeon that Meg takes in, but a swallow, even tinier than the comparatively bulky city birds. She finds it half-frozen in the snow, just like she herself is frozen in her inability to even begin to cope with her situation. Nursing the fragile bird gives Meg the unfamiliar role of a protector, something she does not seem to feel for her infant brother, to whom the narrative impersonally refers as "the baby."[297] Meg sees herself in the swallow, and is determined to keep it safe, just as she herself is actually longing for safety and stability. However fragile swallows may appear in the wild, though, their aerial feeding behavior and the fact that they spend most of their life in flight make them extremely difficult to retain in captivity.[298] The majestic whales, which function as the bridge between life and death, are untouchable, just as the spiritual realm of death and rebirth is untouchable. Yet the swallow, representing courage and freedom, is at the mercy of its keeper. Freedom can be taken away either by another person, just like Meg takes the freedom of the bird, or it can be taken away by oneself, as Meg limits her own freedom through voluntary isolation. Likewise, courage can be nipped in the bud by fear, just as the swallow is in danger of dying due to Meg, whose unhealthy protectiveness stems from her own fear. Both narratives demonstrate the possibility of conveying complex topics

---

295 David Scot, "On the Deror of the Hebrew Scriptures, Translated Swallow in the English Bible," *The Edinburgh New Philosophical Journal 6*, eds. Robert Jameson and William Jardine (Harvard: A. and C. Black, 1829) 93.

296 Harrison 2-3, 6-7.

297 Harrison 12.

298 H. J. de S. Disney, "Notes on Breeding of Welcome Swallows in Captivity." *Australian Zoologist*. Vol. 24.4 (1988): 211.

via the symbolic use of two very different animals. Animals that inspire either admiration (the whales) or sympathy (the swallow) in the reader can be used as powerful symbols, for it is through these emotions that the reader can access topics such as death or freedom more easily. The whales establish a theme of reunion and parting which is tinged by both joy and wistfulness, while the swallow establishes the theme of the gilded cage and the hope of escaping (self-imposed) imprisonment.

5.6. Preserving and Showcasing Culture: Storytelling and Other Traditions in Writing

In many children's books, the representation of certain aspects of a cultural heritage play a central role. Whether it is a spiritual or historical tradition, a specific type of craftsmanship or artistry, or a rendition of the multitude of legends and myths, writing them down, retelling and adapting them, happens for the same reasons that anything is written down. Since the very beginnings of writing, its purpose has always been to help humans remember, and communicate; for example, writing in Ancient Egypt was at first primarily used for administrative and religious purposes. Romans used writing to communicate and record proceedings throughout their vast empire. Medieval Christian monks recorded, copied and distributed the Bible and other religious works for purposes of study and learning. The advantages are obvious. Writing outlasts human memory and allows for the transportation of ideas across great distances, without the simultaneous presence of sender and receiver, narrator and audience. In the context of a multicultural society, writing about specific ethnic traditions follows the same reasons. Cultural knowledge is recorded and disseminated so that it may not be lost. In contemporary Canada, these attempts at preserving cultural heritage in writing have taken on a special importance for minorities, who fear total assimilation into the majority culture with nothing left to call their own. Presenting written traditions, myths and art forms to children, then, is no surprise — passing down customs and stories orally from the old to the young is what societies are built on, and passing down such practices in a multicultural context follows the purpose that the children may take pride in them and continue to pass them on. This intent is very explicitly stated in David Bouchard's *The Dragon New Year: A Chinese Legend*. The grandmother does not merely tell the legend of the New Year celebrations to her grandchild in order to calm or entertain her. Once the little girl has fallen asleep, the narration reveals the grandmother's true intent to the reader: she is hoping to pass the knowledge of the origins of these customs on to her granddaughter, who will one day share them with her children and grandchildren. The story does not merely reveal the reasons for the use of fireworks and the Dragon Dance, but also transports their spiritual significance. Given the rather clear message contained in the text, it is interesting that the book itself is less a retelling of the legend and more a reimagining, weaving different stories together that are not found in the original. Bouchard even includes an appendix to explain various elements he used to create a new story, among them the Dragon Dance, whose origins are unknown, the figure of Buddha, and the figure of the dragon. Unlike Bouchard's reimagining, the original legend only mentions an "old man,"[299] but does not refer to Buddha himself. Neither does the legend paint a dragon as the villain. Nian, or New Year, is presented as either a "(man-eating) sea-monster (serpent)" or a "man-eating monster from the woods,"[300] but not a dragon, as Chinese dragons are generally seen as benevolent deities of water and rainfall, as well as symbols of good fortune, in contrast to their ferocious European counterparts.[301] In the event of a natural disaster, it is believed that humans have angered a dragon and that it needs to be placated.[302] It is unclear what has prompted the author to depict the dragon as a malevolent beast which has to be driven off (or exorcised) rather than pacified, in complete opposition to Chinese mythology. The appendix does not revise this portrayal, but instead states that "the dragon is an unpredictable creature, who can be a strong and loyal friend, but can just as easily be a mortal enemy"[303] and that

299 Jason Huang, "Chinese New Year Legend," *ChinatownConnection.com*, 16 Jan. 2007, 11 Dec. 2009 <http://www.chinatownconnection.com/chinese-new-year-legend.htm>.

300 Yuan Haiwang, *The Magic Lotus Lantern and Other Tales from Han Chinese* (Westport: Libraries Unlimited, 2006) 211.

301 Martin Birnbaum, "Chinese Dragons and the Bay de Halong," *Western Folklore* 11.1 (Jan 1952): 32-33.

302 Birnbaum 35.

303 Bouchard 30.

"it is possible that, one year, back in the mists of time, the celebration of the Chinese New Year began just as I have told it."[304] Given that, as stated in chapter 2.3., the appendix is often used to assure readers (and particularly parents) of the authenticity of the story, tension is created. The explicit goal of the story is to educate children on the Chinese New Year festival — the grandmother character calls the legend an "important story"[305] and states her wish that it be passed on to future generations — yet Bouchard's tale, for all its freely added elements, misrepresents one of the core aspects of Chinese spirituality, namely the dragons, who have always been seen as protectors and symbols of wisdom.

Less conflicting than the reimagining of legends is the depiction of specific artistic practices, which are a central theme in Spalding's book *Solomon's Tree* and Thien's *The Chinese Violin*. The titular violin in Thien's book is an erhu, or two-string fiddle, consisting of a long neck, a small resonator body covered with python skin at the front, and two strings. It is an extremely popular instrument, whose "performance is characterized by subtle contrasts in bowing strength, powerful vibrato, and glissandos."[306] It is a very popular instrument in traditional Chinese music, but has also found its way into the modern Chinese orchestra, as well as the repertoire of modern bands such as the American-based progressive rock group The Hsu-nami, whose songs were featured during the Beijing Summer Olympics in 2008,[307] or the Taiwanese heavy metal group ChthoniC.[308] In Thien's book, the erhu makes an appearance in almost every illustration, and is the one thing that ties Lin Lin to her home in China. She has always loved to listen to her father playing the instrument, but in Canada, its melodies soothe her homesickness. When she eventually learns to play it herself, the violin be-

---

304 Bouchard 31.

305 Bouchard 29.

306 "Erhu," Encyclopædia Britannica Online, 2009, *Encyclopædia Britannica.* 11 Dec. 2009 <http://www.britannica.com/EBchecked/topic/191344/erhu>.

307 "Biography," *The Hsu-nami*, 2009, 11 Dec. 2009 <http://hsu-nami.com/home/biography>.

308 David Frazier, "ChthoniC: A Heavy Metal Alloy of Music and Politics," *NYTimes.com*, 16 Aug. 2007, The New York Times, 11 Dec. 2009 <http:// www.nytimes.com/2007/08/16/arts/16iht-metal.1.7136846.html>.

comes her preferred method of communication, as well. She is depicted playing in the schoolyard, the erhu poised on her thigh, attracting the attention of her classmates, and eventually winning the admiration of an entire auditorium. On the surface, *The Chinese Violin* is about Lin Lin adapting to her new environment in Canada and bridging the physical gap to her home country, but it is also about taking pride in and expressing oneself through one's heritage. Thereby, it also reflects the increasing Canadian acceptance of and fascination with non-European music and instruments — for example, as of February 2009, it is possible for music students at the University of Calgary to take classes in erhu performance.[309]

Solomon's Tree takes up the topic of Tsimshian woodcraft with the carving of ritual masks. Although the narrative does not reflect this at first, Tsimshian art is strongly present throughout the book; for instance, the credits page at the beginning features a painting of Grandmother Moon together with four spirit canoes to symbolize life's journey, and the narrative is decorated with framed strip panels depicting an elongated raven.[310] Woodwork and carving play a very important role in Tsimshian culture, a craft traditionally reserved for men.[311] *Solomon's Tree* depicts in detail the creation of a ritual cedar mask by describing the process from the child's point of view. The illustrations and text show the step-by-step transformation of a log — how it is measured and cut with a chainsaw, how its face is carved with traditional tools, how it is hollowed, smoothed and finally painted. Solomon's uncle is the master carver who allows his nephew to partake in the creation — not only because the wood comes from a log of Solomon's friend, the maple tree, but presumably to introduce him to the craft itself, as well. The boy is certainly enthusiastic, constantly watching his uncle and trying to carry out his instructions. The ending does not only allow Solomon to speak to his favorite maple again, but also demonstrates the significance of the mask in ritual dances and festivals. The uncle fetches his ri-

309 "Erhu Adds International Mix to Music Program," *University of Calgary*, 10 Feb. 2009, 11 Dec. 2009 <http://www.ucalgary.ca/news/utoday/feb10-09/erhu>.

310 Spalding 31.

311 Deanna Nyce, "Aboriginals: Tsimshian – Culture and Religion," *The Encyclopedia of Canada's Peoples*, 2009, Multicultural Canada, 11 Dec. 2009 <http://www.multiculturalcanada.ca/Encyclopedia/A-Z/a12/5>.

tual drum again, just as he did when he first began to carve the mask, and Solomon's entire family joins in the celebration, singing and clapping as Solomon puts on the mask and dances.[312] This authentic depiction of the crafting of a ceremonial mask becomes especially important when one considers the past of the Tsimshian people and First Nations in general — a past that nearly managed to destroy their very way of life. Systematically deprived of their culture through missionary efforts, government assimilation policies, discrimination, forced adoption, and the crimes committed under the guise of the residential school system in the 20th century, the Canadian First Nations communities have suffered a tremendous blow to their health and self-esteem. Language loss and cultural estrangement[313] are only some of the long-term effects, yet thanks to numerous programs and organizations such as the Indian and Northern Affairs Canada (INAC) organization, there has been an increase in language ability and cultural knowledge across First Nations communities.[314] Thus, the engaging, positive depiction of an important aspect of coastal First Nations tradition — the carving of ceremonial masks and the dances during which they are used — in *Solomon's Tree* can only serve to help the promotion of this vital craft and encourage children to take pride in their heritage.

Jeannette Armstrong's *Neekna and Chemai* combines the retelling of legends with the retelling of other cultural practices of the Okanagan people. Whereas Spalding has chosen a distinctly contemporary setting for her tale, Armstrong has chosen the distant past for her purposes — the depiction of a culture untouched by the influence of European settlers. Contrary to the previously mentioned books, which have all focused on only a few specific aspects, Armstrong depicts an Okanagan tribe over the course of an entire year, incorporating a multitude of cultural practices. Likewise, as mentioned in 4.10., the narrative tone of the book is very different, as the book does not focus on developing individual characters, but uses the titular girls,

---

312 Spalding 29-30.

313 Terrellyn Fearn, "A Sense of Belonging: Supporting Healthy Child Development in Aboriginal Families," *Best Start: Ontario's Maternal, Newborn and Early Child Development Resource Center*, 2006. Health Nexus, 11 Dec 2009 <http://www.beststart.org/resources/hlthy_chld_dev/pdf/aboriginal_manual.pdf> 16.

314 Fearn 24.

Neekna and Chemai, as "agents" to transport information about the Okanagan culture. As such, its style is very didactic and laden with facts, attempting to tell rather than show. Yet its purpose remains the same. By depicting the communal lifestyle and child-rearing practices, expositing the specific techniques of weaving used to construct everything from tipi coverings to household appliances such as baskets for cooking, the division of labor, and the nomadic life governed by the cycle of seasons, Armstrong shows a rich culture attuned to the land in which it flowered. The legends told by various characters (usually elders) over the course of the book serve to enhance this representation — the stories of personified plants, which came into being through the sacrifice of ancestral chiefs, showcase the Okanagans' close bond with nature and their communal life, according to which any food gathered was evenly distributed among all members of the tribe.[315] Since the Okanagan, just like all First Nations people, are still suffering from the aftereffects of centuries of colonization and mistreatment, Armstrong's writing is also an important contribution to the growing body of works that depict First Nations culture in a positive manner.

5.7. Westernization and Native Culture

Spalding's, Armstrong's, and Kusugak's stories do not only portray different First Nations cultures, but also portray these cultures at different points in time. As such, one can observe different degrees of Western influence on the cultures in these texts, though not all of them explicitly address the issue. Armstrong's *Neekna and Chemai* is set at an unspecified point in the distant past, but the back cover states that it is happening "before the coming of the white man."[316] This fact is not mentioned anywhere in the text itself, yet it sheds a different light on the proceedings. The Okanagan culture in the story is "ideal," that is to say, free of Euro-Canadian influences. The habits and traditions depicted are authentic and at the core of the tribe. The children are raised communally, educated by older siblings, parents, and grandparents. Poverty seems unknown, as the tribe evenly distributes the spoils of hunting and gathering, and all household appliances, such as

315 Armstrong 32.

316 Armstrong, back cover.

baskets, mats, and weapons, are made by working together. This presents a great contrast to the 20th and 21st centuries, where many aboriginal families are affected by the systematic destruction of their culture, life in the reservations, and the aftereffects of the residential school system. As a result of these forceful changes, the family clan system and communal life have been disrupted, and many First Nations people are struggling with drug and alcohol abuse.[317] Kusugak's *Baseball Bats for Christmas* is set in the less distant past, namely the middle of the 20th century. Since Repulse Bay is so far away, practically on the outskirts of civilization, the influence of Western customs is not yet felt quite as strongly, but, as stated in chapter 4.2., it is unmistakably there. The most obvious symbol is the plaque Kusugak mentions in the opening of his story — a metal plate affixed to a rock by a geological survey team, pinpointing the location of the Arctic Circle. Kusugak describes the scene in a very tongue-in-cheek manner. In a vast world of ice and snow, devoid of most of the comforts a Westerner would come to expect, a survey team has deemed it necessary to leave what amounts to a mark on the Arctic Circle, much to the endless amusement of the local children, who consider the plaque little more than a toy. To them, and probably to most of the adults living in the small town, the plaque has little to no meaning; a serious endeavor of Western science, to catalogue and mark, rendered ridiculous.[318] The influence is felt in numerous other ways, like the British flag flying high when the supply plane is approaching, the checkered shirts and suspender jeans worn by the adults, the Christian mission in charge of educating the children and spreading the Christian belief among people who, for centuries, have had their own gods and celebrations. The Inuit have even adapted the custom of Christmas to something better suited to their own purposes, trading useful objects such as gloves and dogs among each other.[319] The depiction of the Western influence is not necessarily negative — on the surface, it is simply there, just like certain aspects of Inuit culture. Yet the situations Kusugak describes and the narrative tone he assumes, detailing the events from the viewpoint of a precocious little boy, create a certain undercurrent of implicit, humorous ridi-

317 Fearn 23.

318 Kusugak 4.

319 Kusugak 12.

cule of Western attempts at '"civilizing" the Inuit, such as the pompous organ in the little mission church in the middle of nowhere or the singing of English-language Christmas songs despite the fact that few people in the community speak English. Even the Christmas trees, so out of place in a region this far north, are deprived of their purpose, as the children use their branches to carve the titular baseball bats for themselves, and undoubtedly, the remains of the trees would be used by the adults as something other than a festive decoration, as well. *Baseball Bats for Christmas* presents a culture in which the assimilation via Western society is present and felt to some degree, but not yet so advanced as to completely bereave the people of their original customs and traditions.

In contrast, Spalding's book does not focus on the transformation of Aboriginal life like the other two stories do. Set towards the end of the 20th century, the attention is on Solomon's relationship with the tree and his subsequent introduction to his uncle's craft, yet the narrative and illustrations also provide insight into the way First Nations culture and lifestyle have changed. Most of the characters are wearing Western clothing — jeans, t-shirts and baseball caps. Solomon himself is depicted as plump, which could be seen as a reflection of the fact that many Aboriginal children are struggling against weight problems — according to the First Nations Regional Longitudinal Health Survey of 2002/03, more than half (55.2%) of First Nations children partaking in the survey were found to be either overweight or obese.[320] Apart from this, Spalding also weaves together the use of modern and traditional crafts tools in the creation of the mask — the raw wood blocks are cut with chainsaws, while the fine work is performed with traditional chisels and other carving tools. Likewise, Solomon, in a moment of utter pragmatism, does not lay out his nearly finished mask to dry in the sun, but turns to the microwave to hasten the process.[321] In this, *Solomon's Tree* quietly bridges the rift between Western and First Nations culture — the characters' existences are substantially different from the un-

320 *National Aboriginal Health Organization*, "Preliminary Findings of the First Nations Regional Longitudinal Health Survey (RHS) 2002-03: Children's Survey," 4 July 2005, 11 Dec. 2009 <http://www.naho.ca/firstnations/english/documents/2002-03RHSChildPrelimV8.pdf>.

321 Spalding 23.

touched culture Armstrong presents in *Neekna and Chemai*, but they seem to have incorporated both aspects into their lifestyle, and Solomon himself represents a hopeful outlook that the spiritual beliefs and traditional handiwork will live on even in this modern world, with the next generation.

5.8. Historical Events in Children's Literature

Contrary to Armstrong's reimagining of the past in *Neekna and Chemai*, both Kogawa and Wallace take concrete historical occurrences as background for their work. *Naomi's Tree*, based off Kogawa's novel *Obasan*, is set before the same background, namely the outbreak of World War II and the subsequent internment of Japanese Canadian citizens. The picturebook explains the complex political events which led to the dispossession and deportation of more than 22,000 Japanese Canadians in British Columbia[322] by omitting the complex metafictional references that characterize *Obasan,* seeking to explain the situation to very young children in simpler terms: "Great sadness filled the world. And in the Land Across the Sea, families like Naomi's, whose parents or grandparents had come from the Land of Morning, were told that they were enemies. They were all sent away from their homes, their schools, their gardens, their trees, and their friends."[323] The straightforward, concrete language manages to span space and time — losing one's home and friends, the finality of being sent away by a person of authority, are examples that allow readers to imagine the consequences even without the historical background knowledge. Interestingly, the book almost entirely omits Naomi's experience of growing up in the internment camp, and instead chooses to skip ahead to the end of the war. The only hint at Naomi's life in the camp is the illustration on the adjacent page, which depicts Naomi and her brother Stephen working the fields in the British Columbian interior — Naomi shading her eyes and wearily squinting into the distance, the silhouettes of the shacks that served as living accommodations rising in the background.[324] Meanwhile, the narrative focus-

---

322 Ann Gomer Sunahara, *The Politics of Racism: The Uprooting of Japanese Canadians During the Second World War*, 2nd ed. (Ottawa: Ann Sunahara, 2000) 1.

323 Kogawa 12.

324 Kogawa 16.

es on the impossibility of returning home, as Naomi discovers that their house has been sold to strangers, her mother has died, and that "all families like Naomi's were scattered across the country like cherry blossoms in the wind."[325] The complicated workings behind the dispossession of Japanese Canadians and the political decision to forcibly disperse them across Canada[326] are alluded to via the cherry blossoms — flower petals being swept up and dispersed by the wind mean that they are left to an uncertain fate, and it is unlikely that even two blossoms from the same tree will cross paths again. The remainder of the story develops very differently from *Obasan*, whose central theme is the breaking of silence and the unraveling of the deep collective trauma which Gomer Sunahara compares "to that of a rape victim."[327] In contrast, *Naomi's Tree* maintains a more hopeful tone — the difficulty of coming to terms with the past is filtered through Naomi's joyful reunion with her beloved cherry tree, which brings back her memories of happier times. Rather than the shocking ending of *Obasan*, which unveils to Naomi the long-kept secret of her mother's fate (a slow and painful death due to the dropping of the atomic bomb), *Naomi's Tree* chooses to state the mother's death early on in order to focus on the healing process. The long-term effects are naturally still there — the Japanese Canadian community is still in a state of diaspora, and, although redress payments were finally made in 1988,[328] their property remains lost — yet Naomi's personal fate leaves hope that the past can be overcome.

Like Kogawa, Wallace chooses to tell a story of healing amidst aftershocks and continued uncertainty. The problems in *Duncan's Way* — the father's depression, the family's difficult financial situation, the slow death of the community around them — are spurred by the collapse of the Grand Banks codfish stock in the 1990s due to factory fishing. The governmental moratorium on cod fishing in 1992, triggered by the eventual collapse of the cod stock the year before, led to unparalleled mass lay-offs in the Newfoundland fishery business, and, with the end of the income replacement in 1997,

---

325 Kogawa 17.

326 Gomer Sunahara 84.

327 Gomer Sunahara 1.

328 Gomer Sunahara 153.

the slow death of the coastal settlements.[329] Wallace's book illustrates the effects of this tragedy by focusing on the fate of a single family and driving home the magnitude of collapse. Duncan is depicted sitting in a graveyard where his ancestors are buried — all of them fishermen, as the narrative states that this has been their profession for seven generations.[330] What has happened to Duncan's father is not merely a case of unemployment, but the death of a way of life, of a cultural segment, something that has presumably affected many other families in similar ways. The narrative also describes the confusion and perplexity in the wake of the collapse, as politicians and other sources have engaged in a kind of 'blame game,' citing, among other things, the natural seal population as a reason for the disappearance of the cod,[331] or, as Duncan says, the small local fishermen, in a bizarre case of victim-blaming.[332] However, reasons matter very little to Duncan's situation, as he is confronted with the immediate reality of his family's financial ruin, the imminent loss of his home, and his father's state of depression. The story is one of perseverance and adaptation, as Duncan has to find a way that will allow his family to stay and sustain their livelihood — turning away from fishery, but not their love of the sea, by transforming their fishing boat into an ocean-going bakery.

As different as their chosen topics may be, Kogawa and Wallace's reasons for writing children's books on such subjects may be traced to a common factor: silence and lack of acknowledgment. In the case of the crimes committed against Japanese Canadians, it was only in 1988, more than forty years after the end of the Second World War, that the Canadian government issued a public apology and promises of redress.[333] In the case of the

---

329 Gerald Sider, "Between Silences and Culture: A Partisan Anthropology," *Silence: The Currency of Power*, ed. Maria-Luisa Achino-Loeb (New York: Berghahn, 2006) 143.

330 Wallace 2.

331 Tim Hirsch, "Cod's Warning From Newfoundland," *BBC.co.uk*, 16 Dec. 2002, BBC News World Edition, 11 Dec. 2009 <http://news.bbc.co.uk/2/hi/science/nature/2580733.stm>.

332 Wallace 6.

333 "Apology to Japanese Canadians," *CBC Digital Archives*, 22 Sept. 1988, CBC, 11 Dec. 2009 <http://archives.cbc.ca/on_this_day/09/22/>.

cod collapse in the North Atlantic, reports from inshore fishermen as early as 1986 were disregarded in favor of profit, as catches seemed to increase for off-shore trawlers with ever more radical technology at their disposal,[334] something marine biologist George Rose refers to as "hyper-aggression,"[335] a phenomenon that describes fish clustering together when their environment is under pressure. Especially in the case of the Newfoundland collapse, little seems to have changed, as the crab and shrimp populations, which have replaced the cod, are now on the verge of collapse due to overfishing, as well.[336] In both cases, dissimilar though they are, spreading the knowledge of these events via children's books is certainly beneficial, since these publications will not only inform children of events that should never be repeated, but will reach the adult reader, as well.

334 European Union, European Environment Agency, *Late Lessons From Early Warnings: The Precautionary Principle 1896-2000,* by Poul Harremoës et al, eds, 2001, 11 Dec. 2009 http://www.eea.europa.eu/publications/environmental_issue_report_2001_22/Issue_Report_No_22.pdf

335 Hirsch, "Cod's Warning."

336 Canada, Office of the Auditor General of Canada, *Collapse of Snow Crab Fishery in Glace Bay Hole, Nova Scotia,* by Neil P. MacMullin, 26 Oct. 2007, 11 Dec. 2009 <http://www.oag-bvg.gc.ca/internet/English/pet_220_e_29418.html>.

6. Conclusion

This thesis has attempted to highlight the themes of ten selected contemporary Canadian children's picturebooks. These themes, in their parallels and contrasts, present a broad palette of the problems, concerns and views faced and held by contemporary Canadian society — immigration, preservation of cultural practices, the retelling of history and historical injustices, the Westernization which has affected First Nations cultures, and the ways of perceiving and preserving the Canadian nature. The roles of children in these books are varied — children as victims of the difficulties brought on by immigration or historical trauma seeking to transcend their victim role, children who take on great responsibilities to preserve the integrity of their family, children who are protected to the point of isolation, and children who are allowed to grow and act within their capacities, supported by their adult environment. Sometimes, children's books even use child characters as 'story tools,' in order to drive the narrative forward and act either as points of connection for the child reader, or as a possibility to satirize events. The nature of picturebooks, namely the combination and interaction of text and image, opens up new ways of crafting stories, receiving stories, and new layers to examine in stories. Far from robbing the reader of imagination, they provide a challenge by offering both images and text to decode, which requires different skill sets. Especially children, who receive stories so holistically, find a multitude of ways to access complex themes and connect them to their own life experience via picturebooks. Canada's children's literature, especially its picturebook segment, has grown extremely rapidly in a very short span of time, partly due to Canada's colonial history and partly due to the advancement of technology. With the emergence of a sense of national identity and less cost-intensive printing techniques, artistically challenging picturebooks could be produced in order to transport specifically Canadian themes and messages to the young. This has also allowed for increasing representation of First Nations writers, artists, and topics with the foundation of special interests publishers. Above all, however, these developments show how heavily adults are involved in every aspect of children's literature. Adults grant a forum to children's books, are, in the majority of cases, in charge of writing them, and act as judges of their quality and suitability. Moreover, adults tend to read children's books alongside children, and although the reverse can also apply — children reading books intended for older audiences — the child readers do not play as important a role in the production process and critical reception. The implicit adult reader of a children's book does, however, which creates a great variety in narratives and structures, but also great tension among authors and critics. Sometimes, authors feel pressured to cater to the implicit adult audience of children's books, and critics disagree over whether adults can, should, or should not be implicitly addressed. While this adult influence, especially concerning evaluation and readership, is not automatically a negative aspect that should be avoided or eliminated, it does demand openness and insight on part of the adult — not just the writer, but also the adults who are part of the audience, the critics and the scholars. Many things about children's books hinge on the adult perceptions of children and childhood. Whether children are perceived as innocent, whether they are considered victims, commodities, saviors, or growing, developing people who have the capacity to share their experiences and needs with adults, all of these perceptions have a great impact on the way children are portrayed in stories, on the kinds of stories that are written for them, and whether or not they are considered active participants in the reception of these stories, whether their opinions and conclusions are considered, whether or not they are free to discuss and explore their capacities, and, above all, whether they are allowed to enjoy the books written for them, and other kinds of books they may yet discover.

7. Works Cited

Primary Sources

Armstrong, Jeannette C. *Neekna and Chemai*. Penticton: Theytus, 1984.

Bouchard, David. *The Dragon New Year: A Chinese Legend*. Vancouver: Raincoast, 1999.

Gilmore, Rachna. *A Gift for Gita*. Toronto: Second Story, 1998.

Harrison, Troon. *Courage to Fly*. 1st paperback edition. Calgary: Red Deer, 2006.

Kogawa, Joy. *Naomi's Tree*. Markham: Fitzhenry & Whiteside, 2008.

Kusugak, Michael Arvaarluk. *Baseball Bats for Christmas*. Vancouver: Annick, 1990.

McFarlane, Sheryl. *Waiting for the Whales*. Victoria: Orca, 1991.

Spalding, Andrea. *Solomon's Tree*. Victoria: Orca, 2002.

Thien, Madeleine. *The Chinese Violin*. Vancouver: Whitecap, 2002.

Wallace, Ian. *Duncan's Way*. Toronto: Groundwood, 2000.

Secondary Sources

"100 Most Frequently Challenged Books: 1990-2000." *ALA.org*. 28 March 2008. American Library Association. 11 Dec. 2009 <http://www.ala.org/ala/issuesadvcacy/banned/frequentlychallenged/challengedbydecade/1990_2000.cfm>.

Alexander, Christine and Juliet McMaster. "Introduction." *The Child Writer from Austen to Woolf*. Eds. Christine Alexander and Juliet McMaster. Cambridge (UK): Cambridge UP, 2005. 1-10.

Alexander, Christine. "Autobiography and Juvenilia: The Fractured Self in Charlotte Brontë's Early Manuscripts." *The Child Writer from Austen to Woolf*. Eds. Christine Alexander and Juliet McMaster. Cambridge (UK): Cambridge UP, 2005. 154-172.

--. "Nineteenth-century Juvenilia: A Survey." *The Child Writer from Austen to Woolf*. Eds. Christine Alexander and Juliet McMaster. Cambridge (UK): Cambridge UP, 2005. 11-30.

--. "Play and Apprenticeship: The Culture of Family Magazines." *The Child Writer from Austen to Woolf*. Eds. Christine Alexander and Juliet McMaster. Cambridge (UK): Cambridge UP, 2005. 31-50.

Anderson, Kristin J. "Parents or Pop Culture? Children's Heroes and Role Models." *Childhood Education* (Spring 2002). *Findarticles.com*. 11 Dec. 2009. <http://findarticles.com/p/articles/mi_qa3614/is_200204/ai_n9044749/>.

"Apology to Japanese Canadians." *CBC Digital Archives*. 22 Sept. 1988. CBC. 11 Dec. 2009 <http://archives.cbc.ca/on_this_day/09/22/>.

Ariès, Philippe. *Centuries of Childhood: A Social History of Family Life*. Trans. Robert Baldick . New York: Vintage Books, 1962.

Atwood, Margaret. *Survival: A Thematic Guide to Canadian Literature*. Toronto: Anansi, 1972.

Basile, Giambattista. "Sonne, Mond, und Talia." *Das Märchen aller Mär-chen: Der Pentamerone*. Ed. Walter Boehlich. Frankfurt am Main: In-sel, 1982. 45-63.

"Biography." *The Hsu-nami*. 2009. 11 Dec. 2009 <http://hsunami.com/home/biography>.

Birnbaum, Martin. "Chinese Dragons and the Bay de Halong." *Western Folklore* 11.1 (1952): 32-27.

Bissoondath, Neil. *Selling Illusions*: *The Cult of Multiculturalism in Canada*. Toronto: Penguin, 1994.

Brontë, Charlotte. *Jane Eyre*. 1847. London: Penguin, 1994.

Brown, John. *Pet Marjorie: A Story of Child-Life Fifty Years Ago*. Edinburgh: William P. Nimmo, 1864. *GoogleBooks*. 11 Dec. 2009 <http://books.google.ca/books>.

Canada. Office of the Auditor General of Canada. *Collapse of Snow Crab Fishery in Glace Bay Hole, Nova Scotia*. By Neil P. MacMullin. 26

Oct. 2007. 11 Dec. 2009 <http://www.oag-bvg.gc.ca/internet/English/pet_220_e_29418.html>.

Canada. Statistics Canada. *Population by Selected Ethnic Origins, by Province and Territory (2006 Census)*. 20 Nov. 2009. 11 Dec. 2009 <http://www40.statcan.gc.ca/l01/cst01/demo26a-eng.htm>.

Carlson, Ann D. "Concept Books and Young Children." *Ways of Knowing*. 1996. *Rutgers School of Communication and Information*. 15 Nov. 2009 <http://comminfo.rutgers.edu/professional-development/childlit/books/CARLSON.pdf>.

"Challenged Books and Magazines List." *Freedom to Read*. Feb. 2009. Freedom of Expression Committee. 11 Dec. 2009 <http://www.freedomtoread.ca/docs/challenged_books_and_magazines.pdf>.

"Children's Literature." Encyclopædia Britannica Online. 2009. Encyclopædia Britannica. 15 Oct. 2009 <http://www.britannica.com/EBchecked/topic/111289/childrens-literature>.

Choy Lee, Khoon. *Japan — Between Myth and* Reality. Singapore: World Scientific, 1995.

Denney, Jim. Interview. By Jenna Glatzer. Absolute Write. 2007. 11 Dec. 2009 <http://www.absolutewrite.com/novels/jim_denney.htm>.

Disney, H. J. de S. "Notes on Breeding of Welcome Swallows in Captivity." *Australian Zoologist* 24.4 (1988): 211-215.

Driggs Wolfenbarger, Carol, and Lawrence R. Sipe. "A Unique Visual and Literary Art Form: Recent Research on Picturebooks." *Language Arts* 83.3 (2007): 273-280.

Edwards, Gail, and Judith Saltman. "Looking at Ourselves, Looking at Others: Multiculturalism in Canadian Children's Picture Books in English." *Paper Presented to the History of the Book in Canada's Open Conference for Vol. III*. Nov. 2001. 11 Dec. 2009 <http://www.hbic.library.utoronto.ca/vol3edwardssaltman_en.htm>.

Ende, Michael. *Die Unendliche Geschichte*. Stuttgart: K. Thienemanns, 1979.

"Erhu Adds International Mix to Music Program." *University of Calgary.* 10 Feb. 2009. 11 Dec. 2009 <http://www.ucalgary.ca/news/utoday/feb10-09/erhu>.

"Erhu." *Encyclopædia Britannica Online.* 2009. Encyclopædia Britannica. 11 Dec. 2009 <http://www.britannica.com/EBchecked/topic/191344/erhu>.

European Union. European Environment Agency. *Late Lessons From Early Warnings: The Precautionary Principle 1896-2000.* By Poul Harremoës et al, eds. 2001. 11 Dec. 2009 <http://www.eea.europa.eu/publications/environmental_issue_report_2001_22/Issue_Report_No_22.pdf>.

Ewers, Hans-Heino. "Das doppelsinnige Kinderbuch : Erwachsene als Mitleser und als Leser von Kinderliteratur." *Kinderliteratur — Literatur auch für Erwachsene?* Ed. Dagmar Grenz. München: Fink, 1990. 15-24.

"Family Literacy Day World Record Attempt." *ABC Canada.* 2009. ABC Canada Literacy Foundation. 11 Dec. 2009 <http://www.abc-canada.org/fldworldrecord>.

Fearn, Terrellyn. "A Sense of Belonging: Supporting Healthy Child Development in Aboriginal Families." *Best Start: Ontario's Maternal, Newborn and Early Child Development Resource Center.* 2006. Health Nexus. 11 Aug. 2008 <http://www.beststart.org/resources/hlthy_chld_dev/pdf/aboriginal_manual.pdf>.

Frazier, David. "ChthoniC: A Heavy Metal Alloy of Music and Politics." *NY-Times.com.* 16 Aug. 2007. The New York Times. 11 Dec. 2009 < http://www.nytimes.com/2007/08/16/arts/16iht-metal.1.7136846.html >.

Ginsburg, Herbert and Sylvia Opper. *Piaget's Theory of Intellectual Development.* 2nd ed. Englewood Cliffs: Prentice-Hall, 1979.

Gomer Sunahara, Ann. *The Politics of Racism: The Uprooting of Japanese Canadians During the Second World War.* 2nd ed. Ottawa: Ann Sunahara, 2000.

Grimm, Jacob and Wilhelm Grimm, eds. "Dornröschen." *Ausgewählte Kinder- und Hausmärchen.* Stuttgart: Reclam, 1981. 101-106.

Hagge, Linda. "Pentamerone." *Iowa State University*. 22 Jan. 1999. 4 Dec. 2009 <http://www.public.iastate.edu/~lhagge/newpage6.htm>.

Haiwang, Yuan. *The Magic Lotus Lantern and Other Tales from Han Chinese*. Westport: Libraries Unlimited, 2006.

Hirsch, Tim. "Cod's Warning From Newfoundland." *BBC.co.uk*. 16 Dec. 2002. *BBC News World Edition*. 11 Dec. 2009 <http://news.bbc.co.uk/2/hi/science/nature/2580733.stm>.

Hoyte, Carol-Ann. "Book Week Past and Present." *Bookweek.ca*. 2007. TD Canadian Children's Book Week. 11 Dec. 2009 <http://www.bookweek.ca/history>.

Huang, Jason. "Chinese New Year Legend." *ChinatownConnection.com*. 16 Jan. 2007. 11 Dec. 2009 <http://www.chinatownconnection.com/chinese-new-year-legend.htm>.

Hudson, Aïda. "Introduction." *Windows and Words: A Look at Canadian Children's Literature in English*. Eds. Aïda Hudson and Susan-Ann Cooper. Ottawa: Ottawa UP, 2003. 1-9.

Hulbert, Ann. "Wordbound: Child Writers Break Into Print." 12 July 2004. *Slate*. 11 Dec. 2009 <http://www.slate.com/id/2103752/>.

Hunt, Peter. "Defining Children's Literature." *Only Connect: Readings on Children's Literature*. Ed. Sheila A. Egoff. 3rd ed. Toronto: Oxford UP, 1996. 2-17.

Kennedy, Dorothy, and Randy Bouchard. "Native People: Plateau." *The Canadian Encyclopedia*. 2009. Historica Foundation. 4 Dec. 2009 <http://www.thecanadianencyclopedia.com/index.cfm?PgNm=TCE&Params=A1ARTA0009071>.

Kress, Gunther R., and Theo van Leeuwen. *Reading Images: The Grammar of Visual Design*. New York: Routledge, 1996.

Lehr, Susan S. "The Child's Developing Sense of Theme as a Response to Literature." *Reading Research Quarterly* 23.3 (Summer 1988) 337-357.

"Lifestyle of the Okanagan." *Osoyoos Museum*. 19 May 2009. 11 Dec. 2009 <http://osoyoosmuseum.ca/lifestyle_of_the_okanagan.htm>.

Lunn, Janet. "The Picture Book: A Commentary." *Windows and Words*. Eds. Aida Hudson and Susan-Ann Cooper. Ottawa: Ottawa UP, 2003. 185-190.

"Married With Children: Requiem for a Dead Briard." *IMDb*. 2009. The Internet Movie Database. 11 Dec. 2009 <http://www.imdb.com/title/tt0642359>.

McGillis, Roderick. "Canada." *Children's Literature: An Illustrated History*. Ed. Peter Hunt. Oxford: Oxford UP, 1995. 333-343.

Mills, Antonia. "Reincarnation Belief Among North American Indians and Inuit: Context, Distribution, and Variation." *Amerindian Rebirth: Reincarnation Belief Among North American Indians and Inuit*. Eds. Antonia Mills and Richard Slobodin. Toronto: Toronto UP, 1994. 15-37.

National Aboriginal Health Organization. "Preliminary Findings of the First Nations Regional Longitudinal Health Survey (RHS) 2002-03: Children's Survey." 4 July 2005. 4 Dec. 2009 <http://www.naho.ca/firstnations/english/documents/2002-03RHSChildPrelimV8.pdf>.

Natov, Roni. *The Poetics of Childhood*. New York: Routledge, 2006.

Nodelman, Perry. "How Picture Books Work." *Understanding Children's Literature*. 2nd ed. Ed. Peter Hunt. New York: Routledge, 2005. 128-139.

Nyce, Deanna. "Aboriginals: Tsimshian — Culture and Religion." *The Encyclopedia of Canada's Peoples*. 2009. Multicultural Canada. 11 Dec. 2009 <http://www.multiculturalcanada.ca/Encyclopedia/A-Z/a12/5>.

"Pemmican." *Encyclopædia Britannica Online*. 2009. Encyclopædia Britannica. 11 Dec. 2009 <http://www.britannica.com/EBchecked/topic/449526/pemmican>

Perrault, Charles. "La Belle au Bois Dormant." *Contes*. Ed. Marc Soriano. Paris: Flammarion, 1989. 243-253.

Petzold, Dieter. "Multiculturalism in Canadian Children's Books: The Embarrassment of History." *Voices of the Other: Children's Literature and the Postcolonial Context*. Ed. Roderick McGillis. New York: Garland, 2000. 177-192.

Pressler, Mirjam, and Otto H. Frank. *Anne Frank Tagebuch*. Frankfurt am Main: Fischer, 1998.

Saltman, Judith. "Canadian Children's Literature at the Millennium." *Windows and Words: A Look at Canadian Children's Literature in English*. Eds. Aïda Hudson and Susan-Ann Cooper. Ottawa: Ottawa UP, 2003. 23-34.

--. *Modern Canadian Children's Books*. Toronto: Oxford UP, 1987.

Santos, Irene Ramalbo. "Gertrude Stein: The Poet as Master of Repetition." *The Cambridge History of American Literature*. Ed. Sacvan Bercovitch. Vol. 5. Cambridge: Cambridge UP, 2003. 194-216.

Scot, David. "On the Deror of the Hebrew Scriptures, Translated Swallow in the English Bible." *The Edinburgh New Philosophical Journal 6*. Eds. Robert Jameson, and William Jardine. Harvard: A. and C. Black, 1829.

Scott, Carole. "Dual Audience in Picture Books." *Transcending Boundaries: Writing for a Dual Audience of Children and Adults*. Ed. Sandra L. Beckett. New York: Garland, 1999. 99-109.

Shavit, Zohar. "The Double Attribution of Texts for Children and How it Affects Writing for Children." *Transcending Boundaries: Writing for a Dual Audience of Children and Adults*. Ed. Sandra L. Beckett. New York: Garland, 1999. 83-98.

Sider, Gerald. "Between Silences and Culture: A Partisan Anthropology." *Silence: The Currency of Power*. Ed. Maria-Luisa Achino-Loeb. New York: Berghahn, 2006. 141-157.

Sipe, Lawrence R. "Children's Response to Literature: Author, Text, Reader, Context." *Theory into Practice* 38.3 (Summer 1999). 120-129.

Solomon, Michael. "Publishing Children's Picture Books: The Role of Design and Art Direction." *Windows and Words: A Look at Canadian Children's Literature in English*. Eds. Aïda Hudson and Susan-Ann Cooper. Ottawa: Ottawa UP, 2003. 191-200.

Sorin, Reesa, and G. Galloway. "Construct of Childhood: Constructs of Self." *Children Australia* 31.2 (2006): 12-21.

Sorin, Reesa. "Changing Images of Childhood — Reconceptualising Early Childhood Practice." *International Journal of Transitions in Childhood* 1 (2005): 12-21.

Stoodt-Hill, Barbara D., and Linda B. Amspaugh-Corson. *Children's Literature: Discovery of a Lifetime*. Melbourne: Macmillan, 1996.

"TD Grade One Book Giveaway." *Bookweek.ca.* 2009. Canadian Children's Book Week. 11 Dec. 2009 <http://www.bookweek.ca/book-week/td-grade-one-book-giveaway>.

The Canadian Children's Book Center. 2009. CBC. 11 Dec. 2009 <http://www.bookcentre.ca>.

The Neverending Story. Dir. Wolfgang Petersen. Perf. Noah Hathaway, Barret Oliver, and Tami Stronach. Neue Constantin Film, 1984.

Waterston, Elizabeth. *Children's Literature in Canada*. New York: Twayne, 1992.

Wells Rowe, Deborah. "The Literate Potentials of Book-Related Dramatic Play." *Reading Research Quarterly* 33.1 (Jan-Feb-Mar. 1998): 10-35.

Wynne-Jones, Tim. "The Apprehension of Audience: The Difference Between Writing for Adults and Children." *Windows and Words: A Look at Canadian Children's Literature in English*. Eds. Aïda Hudson and Susan-Ann Cooper. Ottawa: Ottawa UP, 2003. 11-21.

Young, Lucie. "Flight of Fantasy." *Telegraph.co.uk*. 27 Jan. 2007. The Daily Telegraph. 11 Dec. 2009 <http://www.telegraph.co.uk/culture/3662784/Flight-of-fantasy.html>.

Zak, Dan. "In Va., Casting About for Mongolian Actors." *WashingtonPost.com*. 2 March 2009. The Washington Post. 11 Dec. 2009 <http://www.washingtonpost.com/wp-dyn/content/article/2009/03/01/AR2009030102088.html>.